Margaret Fuller

MARGARET FULLER
Bluestocking, Romantic, Revolutionary

ELLEN WILSON

FARRAR, STRAUS AND GIROUX / NEW YORK

Library of Congress Cataloging in Publication Data

Wilson, Ellen
Margaret Fuller, bluestocking,
romantic, revolutionary

Bibliography: p. 178 | Includes index.
1. Ossoli, Sarah Margaret Fuller, marchesa d', 1810–1850—
Biography—Juvenile literature.   2. Authors,
American—19th century—Biography—Juvenile literature.
[1. Ossoli, Sarah Margaret Fuller, marchesa d',
1810–1850.   2. Authors, American]   I. Title.
PS2506.W5   818'.3'09   [B]   [92]   77–381
ISBN 0–374–34807–3

Acknowledgment is made to the Houghton Library,
Harvard University, for permission to quote from
two letters of James Nathan, written in 1846.

Frontispiece/*Margaret Fuller*

The Concord Free Public Library,
Concord, Massachusetts

*T*he author wishes to express her gratitude to her son, Douglas C. Wilson, of Amherst, Mass., for suggesting Margaret Fuller as the subject of her present book. She is also indebted for valuable assistance in the research and writing to Mrs. Tess Cederholm, of the Boston Public Library; Dr. Paul John Aiken, of Indiana University; Dr. Wallace E. Williams, of Indiana University, Mrs. Monette Blanchard, of the Providence Athenaeum; Dr. and Mrs. I. J. Kapstein, of Brown University; Dr. Richard M. Cameron, of Boston University; Miss Marcia Moss, of the Concord Free Public Library; Dr. Stuart Sherman, of the John Hay Library, Brown University; Dr. G. Haydn Huntley, of Northwestern University; Dr. William Cagle, of the Lilly Library, Indiana University; Mr. and Mrs. Samuel Rosen, of Nashville, Indiana; and her husband, William E. Wilson. She would like to thank also, for their courteous helpfulness, the staffs of the John Hay Library, the Providence Athenaeum, the Houghton Library of Harvard University, the Concord Free Public Library, and the Indiana University Library.

𝒯HIS, NO TO MORROW HATH, NOR YESTERDAY,
RUNNING IT NEVER RUNS FROM US AWAY,
BUT TRULY KEEPES HIS FIRST, LAST,
EVERLASTING DAY.

Margaret Fuller

1

*I*f Timothy Fuller, like many fathers before and since his time, was disappointed that his first child was not a boy, he celebrated the birth of Sarah Margaret Fuller, May 23, 1810, nevertheless. In her honor he planted two young elms in front of his house in Cambridgeport, Massachusetts, devoutly hoping that his baby daughter would grow to be not only as graceful and beautiful but also as sturdy as the trees themselves.

The father could of course do little or nothing to

give his daughter grace and beauty. She would have to inherit those qualities from her gentle mother, Margaret Crane Fuller. But sturdiness of mind—that was even more important to this lawyer father, and that he could and would give his daughter. He would educate her as rigorously as if she were a son who could go to Harvard and graduate with honors as he himself had done. He would begin as soon as possible.

As a result of her father's intensive daily lessons, Sarah Margaret at the age of four knew her letters and could read. By the time she was six she was translating Latin as well as the older boys in more cultured Cambridge nearby who hoped to enter college.

For the next few years she both loved and hated her lessons. She liked reading about the Romans, because she admired their forthrightness, their courage, and their patriotism. She thought her father was something like her Roman heroes. But she felt he was too much the stern taskmaster, demanding perfect recitations from her, often late at night when he returned from a long day in his law office in Boston.

If she was sleepy, she never dared say so but, with a tremendous effort, kept her eyes open and recited the lessons she had been studying that day. She so feared her father's severe reprimand that she knew she must not make a single mistake. If only he would give her a word of praise now and then, or even a nod of approval, she thought she could go to bed happily and sleep the night through without the nightmares that frightened her so much that she would wake up sobbing, calling desperately for a light.

Sundays were a little better; at least there were no lessons, no recitations. There were family prayers and church in the morning, of course. But after the midday meal Sarah Margaret could wander out into her mother's garden and daydream among the flowers. She thought herself homely. How she longed to be as beautiful as the lilies and the pinks; how she wished she could be as perfect as the rose!

No one ever called her pretty. The only compliment she got was that she was bright. And no one ever told her that to her face. Once or twice she overheard a visiting aunt say to her parents, "Sarah Margaret seems to be brighter than most girls her age. But doesn't she ever play with other children? Why does she always have her nose in a book?" The aunts did not realize that because her father did not send her to school, she did not know any children to play with. Her mother was always too busy with a new baby in the nursery to take her to other homes to play. Books were her only friends, her father her only teacher.

But Timothy Fuller was becoming more and more involved in politics. Although he was thought by many to be narrow and domineering, he was elected to Congress several times by those who knew him to be not only a Puritan and a scholar but an honorable citizen and vigorous patriot. He served in Congress under Monroe and later under his hero, John Quincy Adams.

He first went to Washington when Sarah Margaret was six, arriving for the new year's levee in 1817. Congress was seldom in session for very long at a time, so he did not move his family there but came home to Cambridgeport in the long periods between sessions. Even when in Washington, however, he kept a tight rein on his daughter's educational progress, requiring her to write to him of her studies. Sometimes she wrote her letters in Latin.

One winter Sunday afternoon when her father was back from Washington, eight-year-old Sarah Margaret wandered into his library, where there was a cupboard full of books. She was allowed to browse here, choosing any book that appealed to her—and most of them did appeal to her, because they were not books she had to recite upon. On Sundays there was only one restriction: she was not allowed to read anything so frivolous as a play or a novel.

On this Sunday she pulled out a much-worn book marked simply "Shakespeare"—a book she had never read. Carrying it back to the parlor, where her parents were quietly talking while waiting for the usual Sunday visitation of the aunts, she retreated to a big chair in a corner and was soon lost in the romance of *Romeo and Juliet.*

Oh, the wonder of it! Here was no stern Roman matron or ancient Greek goddess such as she usually read about. Here was a girl of Verona, very beautiful, not yet fourteen years of age and already much loved by the son of such a hostile family that surely tragedy hovered over them both.

Suddenly her father spoke in a voice loud enough to arouse her. "What is that you are reading?"

"Shakespeare," she said simply and went back to the enchanted balcony.

"You know that no one in this house is permitted to read a novel or a play on the Sabbath," said Mr. Fuller sternly. "Take the book back to the shelf where you found it. At once!"

She obeyed promptly, for she knew that there was no use in arguing. But as her parents went on discussing politics and the mundane matters of Cambridgeport, her mind flew back to Italy, where the gallant Romeo and the young Juliet defied their families and declared their undying love.

The aunts finally arrived at the Fuller house, and conversation among the adults became brisk, though still concerned with dull practical affairs. Sarah Margaret slipped out to her father's library and returned unnoticed to her corner in the parlor. Once again she was engulfed in the doomed romance of the star-crossed lovers.

She did not hear when the aunts addressed a question to her. She did not see her mother's reproachful eyes fixed upon her. But she did hear the anger in her father's voice.

"Shakespeare again? Give the book to me." He clapped it shut and said, "Now, go up to your room at once."

She realized that her father was restraining himself in front of the visitors. She knew that she was getting off with a light punishment. In fact, when she flung herself down on her bed, she felt it was no punishment at all. She would get the book again tomorrow.

Meanwhile, she murmured remembered phrases to herself. "This bud of love, by summer's ripening breath,/May prove a beauteous flower when next we meet." And "parting is such sweet sorrow/That I shall say good night till it be morrow." Then her imagination took wing as she tried to invent for herself the rest of the play: what Romeo would say, what Juliet would reply, what brave action would take place in the magic streets of Verona.

After the visitors had gone, her father came up to reason with her. It was not like her to disobey. What had got into her? She should explain herself.

Sarah Margaret was still so much under the spell of the drama that she could not answer her father. How could she explain that she longed to be like the characters in the play, that compared to the dull talk of the people of Cambridgeport, Shakespeare's people spoke sheer poetry? Their lives and loves in sunlit Italy were not humdrum and practical, like those she saw about her in gray, cold New England. Not being able to explain, she kept silent.

Her father had never seen her like this. It was as though she were far away in another world. Baffled, he finally left her, hoping that her going supperless to bed would bring her to her senses.

There were no nightmares for Sarah Margaret that night. She drifted off to dreams, hearing Romeo softly speak: "Sleep dwell upon thine eyes, peace in thy breast."

2

*B*efore she was thirteen, Sarah Margaret begged her family to let her drop the "Sarah" and be called only "Margaret." Her father disapproved. Sarah was his mother's name and the child's baptismal name. As a lawyer, he was not altogether teasing her when he said that to drop half her name would require an act of the General Court. He demanded to know what was behind this strange notion of shortening her name.

Margaret could not bring herself to confess to her

father what she said to a young cousin: "Out upon that Sarah," she had said, half laughing to hide her earnestness. " 'Tis a proper old-maidish name; I will not take it until I am sixty. Then I will sit and knit, look cross and be Miss Sarah Fuller for the rest of my life."

But "Margaret"! There was a poetic name! It was her mother's name. Perhaps if she was called "Margaret," she too would become a gentle lady like her gentle mother, loved by all.

Gradually persuaded, her family fell into the habit of calling her Margaret. "Margaret Fuller," she said to herself. "Now, that is a name I can grow up with."

By the time she was thirteen, Margaret had a younger sister and two younger brothers. The oldest child in the family, she never would forget how, as a three-year-old, she had cried when her first baby sister died. The house was solemn and still, filling with people all in black. Sarah Margaret was put in a high chair and held there by the sad nurse while the clergyman read from the Bible in a sonorous voice. Later, the procession of carriages wended its way to the graveside. Sarah Margaret became a whirling bundle of protest when her infant sister's coffin was being put into the ground. She cried, she stormed, she beat her small fists against the legs of the men who were lowering the small box. Her father caught her up in his arms and held her tight until the ceremony was ended.

Now that Margaret had another sister and two brothers running about the house she was fond of them, but "the little Fullers," as she grew to call them, were too small to be really companionable. Books were still her best friends—not only because her father insisted that she spend her time with her lessons but because she felt that the people in books had more to say to her than her family. The children only prattled, her mother was absorbed in household affairs, and her father was involved in politics.

Earlier, when Margaret was eleven and her father was off in Washington for a long session, he finally decided that his daughter's education needed closer supervision than he could give her at long distance. So she was enrolled in Dr. Park's genteel academy in Boston. The school was attended by young ladies of the first families, all of whom had known each other from babyhood. Margaret admired them and thought them pretty, well-dressed, and sophisticated. They thought her homely, oddly dressed, and countrified, but somehow proud in the way she walked and talked. She tried hard to make friends but was looked upon as an outsider because she came from across the river.

Margaret decided that the only way she could shine among them was in her lessons. Soon she stood second in her class. First was Susan Channing, an older girl, bright, popular, and from an old and important family. Margaret, determined to make not only her father but the whole school proud of her, worked harder than ever to prepare herself for the examinations that were conducted orally before an audience of families and friends.

Margaret wrote to her father:

I am glad you can not witness it . . . Unless I am frightened out of my wits I am sure of History. 'Tis improbable that I shall miss in French and I think my Italian will be all right, but I hardly dare trust geography; the numberless questions on the map disconcert me.

Be assured that I will do my utmost to acquit myself well. I think of nothing else.

Margaret not only acquitted herself well in the exams but outshone everyone else—even Susan Channing. She knew her absent father would be proud of her, but her schoolmates were not. Instead of gathering around Margaret to congratulate her, they rushed to sympathize with Susan, indignant that the new girl had defeated their own champion. Margaret stood forlorn and alone in her empty triumph. When she went home at the end of school, she realized that books were still her best friends, almost her only friends.

She would study at home from now on.

It was not until she was thirteen years old that Margaret suddenly and unexpectedly acquired a true friend who was a person and not a book.

One Sunday, she was sitting in the family pew wishing that for once something strange and rare would happen to break the monotony of the usual service and to rouse her from the lethargy that seemed to afflict most of the congregation on this warm May morning.

She glanced at the family in the next pew. There as usual sat an uninspired family group in their predictably uninspiring row: spinster daughters meekly lined up next to their dull parents. No hope of anything strange and rare there.

Her glance then wandered over other members of the congregation—people she saw Sunday after Sunday—until suddenly she blinked at the sight of a stranger, a young woman. Margaret feasted her eyes on the delicate profile, the elegant bonnet, the gray silk. How still the young woman sat, this vision of loveliness, not in listlessness but in quiet composure, her gloved hands holding the hymnal in her lap. Margaret too sat still, her gaze fixed on the charming newcomer. If only they could meet!

After the service, they did meet. The visitor was a sister of a friend of the Fuller family's and was from

England. The usually talkative Margaret was struck dumb in the presence of the glamorous stranger. "Miss Ellen Kilshaw," Margaret repeated shyly to herself when her parents introduced her.

In the weeks and summer months that followed, Margaret became Miss Ellen's adoring acolyte. The Fullers were happy to entertain the delightful visitor, and Margaret was welcomed in the home of Miss Ellen's relatives. When Miss Ellen painted in oils, Margaret watched every stroke of her brush. When Miss Ellen played the harp, Margaret listened to every note of the angelic music. She had long since found her tongue and, when she and Miss Ellen were alone, poured out in eager confidences her longings and her inmost thoughts to this enchanting visitor from another country, from Shakespeare's country.

For her part, Miss Ellen was charmed by Margaret's childish devotion. The Fuller girl was precocious, bright, and sensitive. She was obviously lonely and needed someone who would listen and understand.

When Mr. Fuller became impatient with his daughter, whose head was filled with "Miss Ellen, nothing but Miss Ellen," Margaret's pride was stirred and she redoubled her efforts at studying just to show her father! Besides, the sooner she finished her lessons, the sooner she could run down the street to the house where Miss Ellen waited to welcome her.

The friendship was a tender one, pleasing to both. In the autumn, when Miss Ellen Kilshaw sailed away, back to England, the parting was sad. The young woman felt that she was leaving a charming young girl who was an original. Margaret felt that she was losing "the angel of her life." She was devastated. She became ill. She fell into melancholy. Nothing she did, no one she saw, appealed to her now that her Miss Ellen was on the other side of the ocean.

Margaret's family were at first impatient and then anxious about this continuing "crush." Letters went back and forth, but the mails were slow and Margaret thought letters a poor substitute for the living, breathing presence of her idol. Nothing could arouse her from her stricken silence.

In anxious desperation, her father finally admitted to himself that he had kept Margaret at home too much. Perhaps a boarding school away from home was the answer. She was such a good student that she could make progress anywhere. She needed to be with other girls of her own age.

So in May of 1824, just before Margaret's fourteenth birthday, she was sent off to the Misses Prescott's school, forty miles away in Groton, Massachusetts. She did not want to go, but she hadn't the energy to rebel. She knew she would hate the Misses Prescott. No one could take the place of Miss Ellen.

But, yes, she would try to make friends at the school. At least it would all be different from her dreary life in Cambridgeport.

3

To no one's surprise, Margaret soon proved to be the best student in the school. But to her own astonishment, she discovered that she was liked by the headmistresses and was becoming popular with the other girls. She was a novelty to them.

The new surroundings, the unexpected friendliness of the teachers and of the girls, stimulated Margaret to respond in a lively fashion. She became transformed—animated, talkative, and full of fun. She entertained the girls with impromptu dramatics.

She danced and recited in the evenings after study hours. She was intoxicated by the informal audiences that gathered in her room to watch and to listen to her. She waved scarves about; she whirled like a dervish; she declaimed and·chanted, mixing up Shakespeare, Greek, and pure nonsense.

Going late to bed, she found it difficult to sleep. Sometimes she walked in her sleep, alarming her teachers. The doctor said simply that she would outgrow the habit. He urged a milk diet.

She organized dramatic performances, always taking the lead. To make herself and the others feel more like professional actresses, she bought a pot of rouge and applied it liberally to their cheeks. Makeup was frowned upon at all other times, but for theatricals the teachers were tolerant. After each performance the girls all scrubbed their cheeks; no nice girl wore rouge.

But because Margaret thought it made her look almost pretty, she began to rouge her cheeks as she dressed for dinner every day. When a few girls ventured to criticize her for this, Margaret thought they were just envious and too timid to follow her example. What she did not realize was that the novelty of Margaret Fuller was beginning to wear off. She did not see that the girls began to be uneasy with her. They sensed a feverish quality in her performances and began to feel that she was almost too melodramatic.

There had always been times when Margaret felt she had to be alone. Abruptly she would plead a headache, turn her back on her friends, and seek solitude, closing her door for a whole evening of study. Then when she wanted them around her again, they always before had eagerly rushed in. But now more and more of them seemed to be holding back.

Why were they drifting away? Margaret had reveled in their admiration, for no one at home had ever praised her. Now she brooded over her schoolmates' growing coolness. Her headaches became more frequent. She rouged her cheeks more defiantly. Frequently she was late to meals or skipped them altogether.

One day in the hour before dinner she stood alone on the school balcony, looking out over the surrounding fields and at the distant hills. It was a tranquil scene and Margaret felt it calm her spirits. She herself became tranquil and serene as she gazed on the great white clouds, the blue hills, and the tall grass gently waving in the fields nearby. She was at peace with herself and with the world.

The dinner bell rang. At first she thought she would ignore the interruption. But then, filled with her new serenity, she went down to her room, changed her dress, and, being late, forgot all about putting rouge on her cheeks. Still in her mood of quiet happiness, Margaret took her place at the long table in the dining hall.

The girl next to her passed her the serving dish, asking if she wanted to help herself. Margaret, still bemused, looked up. She was startled at the sight of the girl's face. On each cheek was a perfectly round, glaring spot of red. Margaret looked across the table. There another friend had painted her cheeks in the same manner. She looked up and down the length of the table, discovering with shock that every girl present had painted her face in a crude parody of Margaret's own custom. She saw quickly that it had been a conspiracy, a plot. Everyone was watching her to see her reaction, suppressing smiles.

Margaret stiffened with pride and gave no indication outwardly that she had noticed anything at all unusual. She talked with her neighbors at the table as she always did. Occasionally she looked around her, hoping to see at least one girl who might have refused to join in the general taunt. But there wasn't one. Even the maids who removed the dishes were tittering and watching her. Worst of all, the teachers themselves seemed to tolerate the hideous practical joke.

Margaret gave no sign that her feelings were in a tumult. An almost unbearable tension built up and up inside her. She felt humiliated and betrayed. When dinner was over and the girls trooped out of the dining room, giggling and making sarcastic remarks, Margaret sat still, a stoic. Finally she rose from her chair, walked slowly up to her room, went inside, locked the door, and fell on the floor in convulsions before she lost consciousness.

When she did not appear at afternoon class, one of the girls was sent to Margaret's room to summon her. She reported to the teacher that Margaret would not answer her knocking, that the door was locked, and that not a sound could be heard from the room. Alarmed teachers finally forced the door open and picked up the unconscious girl, laying her gently on the bed.

When Margaret regained consciousness, she found herself surrounded by tearful, penitent schoolmates who begged her forgiveness for the trick they had played. They had thought of it only as a game to tease her.

Margaret smiled wanly in response as a sign of forgiveness, but deep inside she felt that what she could never forgive was that not one girl had stood up for her, that not one friend had refused to take part in the mocking charade, that not one teacher had protested the humiliating scene.

After that day Margaret seemed utterly subdued.

No longer would she dance or chant before her former audiences. They might try now to be friendly but it was too late. When she had needed them most, every single one of them had betrayed her. They called it a game! Very well, she could play games too.

She concealed her slow-burning resentment as she listened, with apparent sympathy, when girls came to confide in her. But gradually and secretly she took her revenge in insinuations. Did so-and-so know what her so-called friends were saying behind her back? Did this other girl realize what the rest really thought of her? Did the most popular girl in school even suspect that perhaps she was popular only because her family gave her a generous allowance?

Margaret scarcely knew how effectively she was undermining the morale of the whole school. Everyone began to look on everyone else with suspicion and mistrust.

Margaret did not know when the school discovered that she was the troublemaker, the cause of all the dissension. One evening she became aware, however, that something unusual was brewing. There were whispers in corners. Teachers looked grave. The older girls were gathering together in the hallways and turning their backs when Margaret walked past.

After evening prayers, the principal of the school solemnly asked Margaret to come forward to answer certain charges brought against her. Margaret stood by the fireplace facing the whole school. At first she was exhilarated by the drama of it all. This was the end of the game and she would be the winner! Her face flushed, her heart beat fast, her eyes were bright as she began to answer her accusers. In turn, eight older girls, leaders in the school, confronted Margaret with specific charges. Wasn't it true that she had started this particular false rumor, told these specific falsehoods? Could she deny that she had spread slander about certain girls, that she had deliberately set out to ruin their reputations?

At first, Margaret stanchly, even eloquently, defended herself. But as damning evidence relentlessly accumulated against her, she began to falter in her own defense. The enormity of all she had done struck her for the first time. It was no longer a game with the girls that she could win or lose. She realized it was the struggle in herself that she had lost, the struggle between good and evil. She had not only betrayed her friends but she had betrayed herself. She was overwhelmed by guilt and remorse. Again she felt unbearable pressure building up inside.

She looked wildly around her. The principal, sitting at her side, continued to look grave and stern. All the girls seated in rows before her had faces of stone. She saw that one teacher gazed at her with such sorrow, such compassion, that Margaret covered her own eyes with trembling hands. Her shame was more than she could bear. She threw herself down on the floor, striking her head against the iron hearth rail. She lost consciousness.

When she came to, she was utterly despondent. She felt that she had acted so dishonorably that she forfeited all right to friendship, that she had ruined her life. Whenever an anxious classmate or teacher came to her bedside, begging her to sip from a cup of tea or a bowl of soup, Margaret turned her head away and would not—could not—even speak. She wished she were dead.

Each day the teacher who had looked upon her with such compassion when Margaret was on trial pleaded in vain with the stricken girl. Finally, one night, the sympathetic woman burst into tears, saying, "Oh, my child, do not despair! Do not believe that a single fault can mar a whole life! Let me trust you, let me tell you what I have never told anyone." Then she went on to confess a similar crisis in her own girlhood.

As Margaret listened, she was at last aroused from her own hopelessness. If this wonderful teacher had recovered from disgrace to live a life of truth and honor, then there might be hope even for herself.

Without a word but with a look of intense grati-

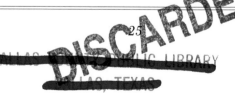

tude, Margaret clasped the hand held out to her and then reached for the nourishing cup.

A penitent Margaret lived out the remainder of the year at the school and returned home "wonderfully instructed." She had learned much—and not only from books.

4

*C*ambridgeport was no longer so dull for Margaret as it had been. Books were still her constant companions as she enthusiastically threw herself into reading French and Italian literature at home. Her pleasure in this reading was doubled because it was all voluntary; she did not have to recite to anyone.

For the study of Greek she attended a private school near her home. But that school, being coeducational, was a new and pleasant experience. It was directed by a Yale graduate, a Mr. Perkins, whose excellent instruction drew bright young people from Cambridge nearby, most of whose fathers were Harvard professors or notable lawyers. Young Oliver Wendell Holmes was one of her fellow students, as was the youthful Richard Henry Dana.

Margaret found she could hold her own with them and was delighted with their companionship. The brightest boys about to enter Harvard obviously enjoyed her lively conversation. Although some of the girls looked on her with wary eyes, the younger girls admired her and even tried to imitate the way she walked and the proud way she carried herself. One girl said they all thought that if they could enter the classroom the way Margaret Fuller did, they could know as much Greek as she did. Even the way she sometimes looked at them with half-closed eyes seemed exotic to them, for they did not realize at first that this was merely a result of her nearsightedness.

She was amused to learn that they wished their mothers would make them hooded cloaks just like the one she had made for herself. They watched her enviously as she filled the hood with books and, instead of wearing the cloak, blithely swung it over her shoulders, walking home with it, books and all.

But Margaret did not forget her much-loved teacher back at the boarding school. She had promised to write often to tell her of her new studies and her life at home. One letter, written in July 1825, gives her daily schedule. Although it was strenuous enough to daunt most adults, fifteen-year-old Margaret took it in her stride because, for her, learning had become a joyous way of life.

Margaret wrote:

You keep me to my promise of giving you some sketch of my pursuits. I rise a little before five, walk an hour, and then practise on the piano till seven, when we breakfast. Next I read French,—Sismondi's Literature of the South of Europe,—till eight, then two or three lectures in Brown's Philosophy. About half-past nine I go to Mr. Perkins's school and study Greek till twelve, when, the school being dismissed, I recite, go home, and practise again till dinner, at two. Sometimes, if the conversation is very agreeable, I lounge for half an hour over the dessert, though rarely so lavish of time. Then, when I can, I read two hours in Italian, but I am often interrupted. At six, I walk, or take a drive. Before going to bed, I play or sing, for half an hour or so, to make all sleepy, and, about eleven, retire to write a little while in my journal, exercises on what I have read, or a series of characteristics which I am filling up according to advice. Thus, you see, I am learning Greek, and making acquaintance with metaphysics, and French and Italian literature.

An ardent spirit was what Margaret brought to everything she did. When she was sixteen, her father moved the family from prosaic Cambridgeport to the far more gracious and stimulating atmosphere of Cambridge itself. To Margaret's delight they moved into the fine eighteenth-century mansion on Dana Hill that had once been the home of Francis Dana, the first United States Ambassador to Russia.

Margaret suspected that her father had some ambition to serve in a European diplomatic post himself. He had been President John Quincy Adams's campaign manager in the recent successful election. Shouldn't he be rewarded by some such foreign assignment? What a splendid thing it would be if her father were made ambassador to England! Then she could explore Shakespeare's country. She admitted to herself that she was scarcely ready for the Court of St. James's, but surely she was less awkward than she used to be. And with all her reading of French and Italian literature, mightn't she even fit into life in France or Italy?

Books would always be important to her, but now in pursuit of social graces she was glad to go frequently to small parties in Cambridge, where Harvard students and even their professors apparently found her interesting to talk to. Those of the famous Class of 1829, of which Oliver Wendell Holmes and other men of future renown were members, treated her as though she were eighteen or nineteen instead of just sixteen. She not only sounded more mature, she looked it too.

By now she was almost reconciled to not being beautiful. "Very well then," she said to herself, "I will be ugly and bright."

She wasn't ugly. Many did think her plain. But she became animated when involved in lively conversation. She could be gay and witty; her nearsighted eyes sparkled; she made pleasing gestures with her hands. Then most of her listeners forgot her frizzy curls, her too-florid complexion, her rather unbecoming clothes. At such times Margaret herself forgot the large bosom that usually embarrassed her.

Her new social life was to come to a heady climax when her father planned a dinner and ball on Dana Hill for his friend John Quincy Adams, President of the United States.

On the Fourth of July 1826, a semicentennial celebration swept the entire country. In Boston and Cambridge bells were rung and fireworks starred the sky; all Americans rejoiced in fifty years of independence. But the next day all were saddened by the news of a startling coincidence: both the third President, Thomas Jefferson, and the senior John Adams, second President, had died on Independence Day.

John Quincy Adams hastened to his father's home in New England to look after the former President's affairs. Later, he gravely accepted Mr. Fuller's invitation to spend an evening at Dana Hall before returning to Washington.

Upon his acceptance the Fuller household was thrown into a frenzy of preparations. For Margaret this was to be a splendid social debut. For her father, now out of Congress and in the state legislature, it was to be an impressive way of reviving and advancing his political career. Surely a foreign post would be offered to him when the President saw how brilliantly his Yankee compatriot could entertain in his own fine mansion.

Everybody who was anybody was invited to meet the President at the reception and ball that would follow a small select dinner. The most distinguished members of the Harvard faculty, the most prominent Bostonians, the most loyal politicians and their wives —all eagerly accepted the Fullers' invitation. Margaret was allowed to ask a score or more of young people to come and join in the dancing. She admitted to her father that she was "passionately fond of dancing" and began sewing her new ball gown of bright-pink silk and white muslin.

Self-effacing Mrs. Fuller stayed in the background as her husband took charge of all preparations for the great event. He was the one to decide on the dinner menu, the punch, the oyster supper for midnight. It was he who arranged for the music, the tall tapers that lighted every corner of the handsome house. He hired the waiters, the additional kitchen help. He chose the wines to accompany the small formal dinner. He was even the one to approve Margaret's newly finished gown, overlayed with muslin. He was everywhere, lavishly spending money and effort on what he knew would be a triumphant evening's entertainment.

On the great night, Mr. Fuller greeted the honored guest, then presented to the President his gentle wife, his vivacious daughter, and all the young Fullers dressed in their Sunday best: There was Eugene, the oldest, and to Margaret the most companionable of the brothers; there was William Henry, sturdy but with small interest in his studies; there was little sister Ellen, a beautiful child; and there were Arthur and Richard, the youngest, still in rompers. The children were dismissed as other guests arrived.

Mrs. Adams had sent her regrets because she was indisposed. But the dignified Mr. Adams responded graciously enough to his host, and the distinguished guests gathered around the dinner table.

Margaret, seated next to the President, remembered her resolve to overcome what she called her lack of "intuitive tact and polish." She did her best to entertain the great man, although she found him rather formidable. Wait until the dancing begins, she thought. Then he may relax, and so shall I.

But at the conclusion of the magnificent dinner, the President unexpectedly made his farewells. "My wife is ailing," he said, "and I must return to her." There was nothing for the Fullers to do but call his carriage, press his hand in farewell, and hold heads high while facing the vast numbers of other guests rolling up in their carriages to the front door on Dana Hill "to meet the President."

That night Margaret felt sorriest for her father. Apparently there was to be no diplomatic post for him. There was to be no England, no France or Italy for her. But meanwhile, for her father's sake, she must try to save the party from complete disaster. There was no guest of honor to lend luster to the evening, so she herself must try to shine. And shine she did.

She talked to everybody. And every man from the dignified president of Harvard to the most awkward freshman danced with the spirited young hostess. Her witty sallies delighted them, and she was easily the belle of the ball.

Not everyone succumbed to her charm, however. One of the matrons, a professor's dour wife, watching her, later gave this jaundiced report. Margaret had "a very plain face, half-shut eyes, and hair curled all over her head; she was laced so tightly . . . by reason of stoutness, that she had to hold her arms back as if they were pinioned; she was dressed in a badly-cut, low-necked pink silk, with white muslin over it; and she danced quadrilles very awkwardly, being so near-sighted that she could hardly see her partner."

A more sympathetic faculty wife, Mrs. John Farrar, noticed some of the same defects in Margaret's appearance but was so taken with the girl's personality that she resolved to help her overcome her faults of dress and manner. This she did later, after the two had become good friends.

But that evening Margaret, unconscious of any criticism, had a wonderful time and gave her guests a wonderful time. Many of them almost forgot their disappointment in not meeting the President. They felt that at least they had met a most interesting young woman.

5

*M*argaret once wrote in her journal: "I remembered how as a little child I had stopped myself
on the stairs and asked how I came here? How is it
that I seem to be this Margaret Fuller? What does it
mean? What shall I do about it?"

At another time, she wrote: "Very early in life I
knew that the only object in life was to grow." She
intensely wanted to grow in mind. That meant not
just gathering scholarly information. She wished to

encompass all knowledge with the purpose of understanding life and her own place in it.

For the next few years in Cambridge, Margaret's life was not so much a series of exterior events as it was a time of inner growth. She continued to read avidly, discovering Goethe's writings through her good friends Frederick Henry Hedge and James Freeman Clarke, who were among the first to bring German literature to America. She taught herself German and had long stimulating conversations with these young men about her new hero, Goethe, and his philosophy.

Margaret also made many new friends among the women of Cambridge. She adored Mrs. Farrar, wife of the professor of astronomy, because she was an accomplished and gracious lady who had lived abroad. But she loved her even more because of her early and kindly interest in Margaret's social development. The childless Mrs. Farrar eagerly took this intelligent girl under her wing. Tactfully she persuaded Margaret to abandon the ugly curl papers that resulted in her frizzy, corkscrew curls, helping her find simpler ways of arranging her hair. She suggested colors more becoming than pink and introduced her own dressmaker, who taught Margaret to adapt patterns so as to minimize her overdeveloped bosom and enhance her graceful neck and lovely shoulders. Mrs. Farrar also undertook to smooth out some of Margaret's awkward and abrupt manners.

There was no swift transformation. In fact, throughout her life Margaret found that there were always some people who mistook her self-confidence for egotism, her impatience with mediocrity for superciliousness, her brilliant conversation for exhibitionism. There were even a few who compared the graceful turning of her head on her swanlike neck to the sinuous movements of a snake. But there were very few who did not eventually fall under the binding spell of her eager spirit.

One of these early friends was a visiting relative of Mrs. Farrar's, young Anna Barker, a beauty from New Orleans who instantly drew all the young men of Harvard about her. Far from being jealous, Margaret herself became devoted to Miss Barker, rejoicing in the girl's beauty and in her friendship. In fact, she looked upon Anna as a model not only of goodness but of grace, qualities that she herself longed to possess.

The Farrars' house became a second home to Margaret, and she was included in all family activities. There was some talk of Mr. and Mrs. Farrar's taking the two girls on a trip with them, perhaps even abroad sometime. Margaret was almost delirious with delight at such a prospect; there was so much she could learn in Europe. Now if only her father would let her go.

Mr. Fuller only half listened to her excited requests. After all, there was no hurry since there was no definite plan as yet. Besides, he had more serious problems on his mind. If he had had any lingering hopes for advancement under John Quincy Adams, those hopes were completely wrecked when, in 1828, Adams himself was swept out of office by the popular Andrew Jackson. Bitterly disappointed, Mr. Fuller grew more and more taciturn. His gloom filled the house. What folly it had been for him to spend money and hopes on that party for President Adams and on his own political career. His law practice was dwindling. His finances were in such straits that he had to give up Dana Hill. Moving his family temporarily to Brattle Hall, he finally in 1833 settled them on a farm outside of Groton.

For twenty-three-year-old Margaret the move was exile. To leave Cambridge, where she was surrounded by stimulating friends, where every day she could discuss her reading with intellectuals, where she was truly inspired by the sermons of young Ralph Waldo Emerson, where libraries were always at hand, where people like the Farrars opened up new worlds of music, art, and the prospect of travel—to leave all this, she felt, was to leave life itself.

"I confess," wrote Margaret later, "I greeted our new home with a flood of bitter tears."

The tears were for herself. But they were soon shed too for ten-year-old Arthur, who, playing with a toy cannon, was so badly injured that he was threatened with the loss of an eye.

In the days and weeks that followed, Margaret nursed the stricken boy. Upon his recovery, she immersed herself in teaching all the young Fullers. The two oldest boys had left home: Eugene was a student at Harvard and William Henry, with no scholarly ambitions, was apprenticed to a merchant on Avon Place in Boston. But the education of blooming young Ellen in her teens was Margaret's special charge. The younger boys—Arthur, Richard, and the smallest, not very bright member of the family, Lloyd—also became their older sister's pupils when they were not helping their father with farm chores.

Margaret tried to submerge her own personal rebellion by attempting to kindle in her sister and brothers the same love of knowledge that she herself had. She was not so severe an instructor as her father had been with her. But she found it tedious to teach them, even though she grew to love them. She wrote: "Five and often eight hours of the twenty-four, I give lessons in Latin, English, French, Geography and History—a somewhat fatiguing charge for one of my impatient disposition." She did all the sewing for the four young ones, too, and what with helping her "angelic" but ailing mother with household duties she had very little time to herself.

She did not try to hide from her father her unhappiness in their new life. In an effort to placate her, Mr. Fuller built a rustic shelter in a small clump of woods near the house. He urged her to use it as a retreat when she needed to be alone with her thoughts. But she scarcely thanked him, and she never used it. The weather was often raw and cold, the little farm seemed barren and bleak, and Margaret usually had no time until late at night to be alone with her thoughts. Then she retreated to her bedroom to read half the night, to study, and to write letters to those fortunate friends who still lived in that mecca of her dreams, Cambridge—a town only forty miles away but seeming as far distant as London or Rome.

The only interest that drew her father and Margaret at all close was their reading of American history together, especially the correspondence of Thomas Jefferson. An unexpected tie was their common indignation over an article in the *North American Review* for October 1834, by George Bancroft, the well-known historian, entitled "Slavery in Rome." Margaret so disagreed with Bancroft's low opinion of Brutus that with her father's encouragement she wrote a rebuttal in defense of Brutus. She sent her letter to Boston's leading newspaper, *The Daily Advertiser.* Fearing that they would not take her argument seriously if they knew it was from a woman in her early twenties, she signed it mischievously with the misleading initial "J."

It promptly appeared in the paper, taking up an entire column. Her first published piece! No matter that no one knew it was by Margaret Fuller; *she* knew. She and her father were again elated when another writer entered the fray, defending Bancroft. His letter was from Salem and signed "H." What a compliment it was to be answered seriously by Nathaniel Hawthorne! Perhaps a writing career was what lay ahead for Margaret? Until now her writing had been confined to her private journal and personal letters and a few poems she had shown only to close friends. Now, however, as she clipped her article from the newspaper, her ambitions were stirred. Someday she would write something that she would sign, not timidly with a wrong initial, but boldly "Margaret Fuller."

Life on the farm, however, continued to be frustrating, full of tedious tasks and endless burdens. Margaret's head ached constantly. She drove herself so hard that she finally broke down completely. She took to her bed with what the doctor called "brain fever." For nine long days and longer nights her family feared she would die. Her mother nursed her "like an angel." Her father was so distressed that when he came to her bedside one morning he tried for the first time to express his feelings toward her.

"My dear, I have been thinking of you in the night, and I cannot remember that you have any *faults*. You have defects, as all mortals have, but I do not know that you have a single fault."

From her undemonstrative father this was a tribute that moved her to tears. When Margaret recovered, she felt closer to both her parents than she ever had.

In the summer of 1835 Mrs. Farrar persuaded the Fullers to let their daughter visit her. Another house guest was Miss Harriet Martineau, a celebrated author who had come from England to see how well Americans were living up to their early promise.

Margaret quickly lost her awe of the famous visitor. She wrote: "Miss Martineau received me so kindly as to banish all embarrassment at once." They took to each other—this Englishwoman only eight years older than Margaret, already known on two continents, and the young American who longed for wider horizons. Miss Martineau, who was interviewing as many people as possible—from the President on down to the lowliest plantation slave—found in

Margaret the ideal young American woman-pioneer in both her thinking and her conversation. She urged Margaret to come to England with the Farrars the following year, when she would introduce them to Thomas Carlyle and other literary lights. A heady prospect!

Meanwhile, the Farrars invited Margaret to go with them on a shorter excursion closer to home. If only her father would let her accept! She wrote to him:

And now I have something to tell you which I hope, oh, I HOPE *will give you as much pleasure as it does me. Mr. and Mrs. Farrar propose taking me, with several other delightful persons, to Trenton Falls this summer. The plan is to set out about the 20th of July, go on to New York, then up the North River to West Point,—pass a day there; then to Catskill,—pass a day there; then on to Trenton, and devote a week to that beautiful scenery. I said I had scarcely a doubt of your consent, as you had said several times last winter you should like me to take a pleasant journey this summer. Oh, I cannot describe the positive ecstasy with which I think of this journey! to see the North River at last, and in such society! Oh, do sympathize with me! do feel about it as I do! The positive expenses of the journey we have computed at forty-seven dollars; I shall want ten more for spending money,—but you will not think of the money, will you? I would rather you would take two hundred dollars from my portion, than feel even the least unwilling. Will you not write to me immediately, and say you love me, and are very glad I am to be so happy???*

When her father gave his consent, the trip proved to be all that Margaret had hoped for. Her excitement and pleasure were due not only to the wonders of travel and the magnificence of the scenery along the Hudson (the North River) but to the fact that she was sharing these joys with such congenial company. Her dear friends the Farrars and young Sam Ward, a banker's son who was far more interested in art and literature than in banking, composed the party. Margaret fell half in love with "Mr. Ward who has been all kindness." She felt that it was he who opened her eyes to all the poignant joys of nature. Later she wrote a poem about their return called "Sunset After Leaving New York." The last two lines show her romantic attachment:

All this we two could see, together feel;
Since then no more alone at Nature's shrine I kneel.

That autumn, however, Margaret had to abandon all

dreams of romance and further travel, and all personal ambition.

Her father died suddenly of cholera October 1, 1835.

Her mother, timid by nature and overcome by grief, turned helplessly to her daughter. Margaret now had to act as head of the family. She gathered the children around her father's bier and vowed that she would care for them, educate them, and by fidelity to them atone for any lack of gratitude to their father.

She wrote in her journal: "I have prayed to God that my duty may now be the first object and self set aside. May I have light and strength to do what is right . . . for my mother, brothers and sister."

6

$\mathcal{M}$r. Fuller left no will. His financial affairs were in a tangle, and Uncle Abraham Fuller, a testy bachelor brother, as nearest male relative, was appointed executor.

Margaret wrote:

I have often had reason to regret being of the softer sex, and never more than now. If I were an eldest son I could be guardian of my brothers and sister, administer the estate, and really become the head of my family.

For months, until the estate was settled, there was very little ready cash. Fortunately, Eugene and William Henry, away from home, were now almost self-supporting. Margaret continued to teach the younger Fullers; she took care of her mother and lived as economically as possible on the farm.

She learned that the family would eventually inherit about twenty thousand dollars, her mother receiving the widow's third and the rest being divided among the seven children—not enough to guarantee a comfortable future. Margaret's dearest wish for Ellen was that she be sent to a good school, but she had to argue vehemently with Uncle Abraham, who thought it a waste of money to spend a dollar on educating a female. It was only when Margaret said she would give up her own inheritance if necessary, to further Ellen's education, that her uncle, refusing to let her do that, promised that Ellen's money could be used for schooling.

Margaret tried to stifle her own heart's desire, which was to spend her share of the inheritance on that longed-for trip to Europe. Never again, she thought, would there be such a blissful opportunity as the one the Farrars were offering her. They, with Miss Martineau, were to sail in the summer to England, and the three of them urged Margaret to go with them. As a house guest of the famous Miss Martineau, Margaret would have introductions to the most distinguished literary figures of the time. What an education such a trip would be for her! She had read widely in foreign literature but had never set foot on foreign soil. Margaret yearned to go, longed to say yes. All that winter she struggled with herself. But in the end she knew she must sacrifice her dream; she would stay to look after her family.

When her friends finally sailed without her, Margaret would have been desolate if she had not found a new friend and hero, Ralph Waldo Emerson. Miss Martineau had arranged their meeting. On a visit to Emerson's house in Concord, the Englishwoman constantly sang Margaret's praises. She spoke of her sacrifice in giving up her cherished plan of going abroad. She called Margaret a genius and a brilliant conversationalist, who had long admired Mr. Emerson from afar. All of this surprised her host, who had heard Miss Fuller spoken of by some as a sarcastic bluestocking and a supercilious scholar. Miss Martineau was convincing, however, and persuaded the Emersons to seek Margaret out and make her acquaintance. Newly married Lidian Emerson, Ralph Waldo Emerson's second wife, duly wrote a note inviting Miss Fuller to pay them a fortnight's visit in July.

Harriet Martineau

By permission of the Houghton Library,
Harvard University

Ralph Waldo Emerson,
"The Rainbow Portrait," by David Scott

The Concord Free Public Library,
Concord, Massachusetts

Margaret was delighted to accept. Concord wasn't Europe, but with Mr. Emerson living there it was a good substitute. She and her Cambridge friends had gone whenever they could to hear this man, who was becoming famous as the "young people's preacher." He resigned his regular pulpit in Boston, turning his back on conventional religion, and lectured on a new philosophy, later to be called Transcendentalism, based on man's relation to nature. Margaret responded to his eloquent talk of self-reliance, individualism, and self-culture. And now she had the chance to meet and talk with this great and wise man under his own roof.

Margaret packed her most becoming clothes and in high anticipation rode the post chaise to Concord. She was warmly greeted by the Emersons, but at first things did not go well. Emerson was put off by her trick of opening and shutting her eyelids, the rather nasal tone of her voice, the effect of her manners. She seemed excited and overeager to please, as indeed she was. Her host retired to the quiet of his study as soon as he could. Later he wrote: "She made me laugh more than I liked." He was used to solitude and scarcely knew how to respond to this vivacious creature who seemed to fill the house with talk and laughter.

Both Emerson's wife and his mother, however,

were at once captivated by their entertaining guest. And it wasn't long before Emerson himself capitulated. He wrote:

She studied my tastes, piqued and amused me, challenged frankness by frankness, and did not conceal the good opinion of me she brought with her, nor her wish to please. She was curious to know my opinions and experiences. Of course, it was impossible long to hold out against such an assault. She had an incredible variety of anecdotes, and the readiest wit . . . and the eyes which were so plain at first, soon swam with fun and drolleries, and the very tides of joy and superabundant life.

Margaret settled into the routine of the Concord household. She realized that Emerson needed his mornings for meditation and study. That suited her very well, for she could stay in her own room, reading, writing poetry, making entries in her journal, or writing letters, particularly to her mother and sister. She assured them that she would come home immediately if they summoned her for any sudden need. She appreciated their letting her have this fortnight with these new friends who were so good to her and who had invited her to stay for a third week. She said, "The baby here is beautiful. I play with him a good deal."

On fair afternoons Emerson was pleased to take Margaret on his favorite walks in and out of Concord, along the banks of the slow-moving Assabet River, or around the edge of serene Walden Pond. On these unhurried excursions they sometimes fell silent; then Margaret felt herself joining Emerson in deep communion with nature. They always returned to be with the ladies of the house for talk and tea in the large, cool dining room. There she could play with baby Waldo, fresh from his afternoon nap and gurgling with delight. These happy domestic scenes moved Margaret strangely. Would she herself ever know the joy of being a wife and mother?

But in the evenings Margaret put aside these longings and eagerly joined Emerson in his library for stimulating talk about everything—religion, poetry, love, even the place of women in America as compared to their role in the French Revolution. Emerson was astonished at the scope of her reading, the range of her thinking.

When she confessed to anxiety as to how she could support her own family, Emerson introduced her to Amos Bronson Alcott, who offered her the position of teaching Latin and French in his Temple school in Boston. She accepted. After all, she had spent many years teaching her brothers and sister just for love. Now a small regular salary would make a dif-

Ralph Waldo Emerson's house in
Concord, Massachusetts, as it looked
when Margaret Fuller was a visitor

The Concord Free Public Library,
Concord, Massachusetts

ference in the way she could help her mother.

Mr. Alcott's school was as different from most schools as Bronson Alcott himself was different from most headmasters. He thought that educating children was not a matter of stuffing their heads with information but a matter of drawing them out in conversation about their studies. He thought that every child was capable of genius, and that the spiritual development of each was of the greatest importance. Margaret thought the school, set up in the Masonic Temple, was an attractive place. There were individual chairs and desks for the children—not the old rows of immovable benches. There were pictures on the walls; a portrait of Dr. William Ellery Channing, Boston's most famous religious leader, had the place of honor. Busts of famous men were placed around the room. There was never any physical punishment of pupils; they were encouraged to discipline themselves, and recreation was a part of each day's program.

Margaret's informal but intensive method of teaching "the little Fullers" worked very well here. That winter she had her pupils reading French and Latin in no time. Her own enthusiasm and dedication were contagious. Anna and Louisa May Alcott were among those who became devoted to her.

But to Mr. Alcott the most important contribution

Margaret made was to record the conversations he himself had with the children, drawing them out on the Gospels. Far from being puritanical, these conversations were very free—so free that when they were published they created a storm of protest. Newspapers denounced the school, and Mr. Alcott's little book was called "one third absurd, one third blasphemous, and one third obscene."

Emerson warmly defended Mr. Alcott, saying that he was only trying to make children think. Margaret too defended him, because she knew he was an innocent, almost saintly educator of the young, although she realized how impractical he often was. When parents started withdrawing their children from the experimental school, she could see that her days of teaching there were numbered.

Meanwhile, she had organized outside classes of young ladies, teaching them German and Italian for very little money. In addition she tutored a few private pupils, the most challenging of whom was a young blind boy. In ten weeks Margaret taught him Latin and read to him a history of England and the historical plays of Shakespeare.

One evening each week Margaret went to Dr. Channing's house to translate German authors for him. She wrote in a letter to a friend that she found the great man rather more deliberate in taking in subjects than "feminine people, with our habits of ducking, diving, or flying for truth." She was fair enough to add: "Doubtless, however, he makes better use of what he gets . . . There is much more talking than reading; and I like talking with him."

Thursday nights were starred in her calendar. Then Margaret went eagerly with most of Boston's intellectuals to hear Mr. Emerson lecture. With others she fell under the spell of his golden voice as he called upon all young people to find something "great and good to do with their whole hearts."

It was an exciting but wearing winter for Margaret. She loved the stimulus of life in Boston, but found she had taken on too much. In addition to her many hours of teaching, she kept up her own exhaustive reading in her room at night and seriously tried to work on the life of Goethe that she had long wanted to write. Her health again threatened to give way, and she welcomed the end of school and did not mind, except for his sake, that Mr. Alcott could not afford to employ her for another year. She had proved to herself that she could earn some, if not enough, money for her family. She would go back to the farm in Groton now to rest and recover. Perhaps later she could work on her life of Goethe. That, she thought, would be something great and good she could do with her whole heart.

Amos Bronson Alcott

By permission of the Houghton Library,
Harvard University

Moreover, George Ripley, who was publishing a series of studies of foreign literature, had offered to publish Margaret's *Goethe* when she finished it. That would bring her not only deep personal satisfaction but also some money— not much perhaps, but something.

Unexpectedly, she was offered a teaching position in a new school in Providence, Rhode Island. Her salary would be more than she had ever made— $1,000 a year. And better still, she would teach only four hours a day, from eight-thirty to twelve-thirty. That should leave her afternoons free to devote to her writing.

She was sorry to leave Boston, that "Athens of America," but she discovered that Providence had its own quality. Founded by Roger Williams, it had a tradition of religious freedom. Margaret liked walking along streets named Benefit, Benevolent, and Hope. The first families of Providence were merchants, taking their cue from New York rather than Boston. However, Margaret learned that the already long-established college on the hill, Brown, and the new Athenaeum Library contributed to the cultural life of the town.

The Green Street Academy, where she taught, was in a beautiful new building like a Greek temple. The headmaster was Colonel Hiram Fuller—no relation to Margaret's family. She wrote to a friend that "Mr. Fuller is as unlike as possible to Mr. Alcott. He has neither his poetic beauty nor his practical defects." He was like Bronson Alcott only in that he admired Margaret Fuller and had sought her out as his assistant and his principal teacher.

The new academy was dedicated on June 10, 1837, with Ralph Waldo Emerson coming from Concord to give the main address. Apparently Margaret was one of the few in the audience to understand and appreciate his talk. The Providence *Journal* wrote that Emerson's thoughts on education were "so transcendental that they were scarcely intelligible."

Margaret stayed for two years teaching sixty "miserably prepared" children. She was a great success as a teacher, but began to feel that as a life work teaching was too limiting. She involved herself somewhat in activities in the town. She attended a Whig caucus meeting—to Colonel Fuller's horror, for women were not encouraged to show an interest in politics or government. When a French man-of-war visited the United States and dropped anchor in Narragansett Bay, Margaret went aboard to explore. She was fascinated by the workings of the ship and wrote to one of her brothers: "I thought I much should like to command such a vessel despite all the hardships and privations of such a situation."

At the end of her second year at the school, Margaret resigned, worn out from her labors and with no manuscript of her life of Goethe to offer a publisher. She had translated Johann Eckermann's *Conversations with Goethe*, however, and George Ripley was glad to publish it. Having learned that she hadn't the time or energy to write as she wanted to while teaching, she wrote to Emerson: "I do not wish to teach again at all." But that winter on the farm in Groton she hit upon a plan that she hoped and prayed would be the answer to her problem of earning a living.

7

When Mrs. Fuller sold the farm in the spring
of 1839 and Margaret moved the family to a delightful rural suburb of Boston called Jamaica Plain, she
was now close enough to the city to put her plan into
action. The plan, quite simply, was to gather together
the most intelligent women of the area and hold conversations on various interesting and stimulating
topics.

Margaret felt keenly that women had no clubs of
their own, that the infant Mount Holyoke was the
only college they could attend, that there were no

professions open to them except teaching, an honorable occupation but one in which they dealt only with young and immature minds. There ought to be a way, she thought, for women to continue their education, to keep their minds alive and growing. Perhaps all they needed was someone to guide and counsel them, someone whose own education had never ceased, someone who could talk eloquently of ideas and encourage them to converse on subjects more challenging than their domestic crises in kitchen and nursery.

Margaret knew without false modesty that she could be that person. Hadn't she been the first woman to be accepted into the discussions of the men's Transcendental Club? Hadn't Emerson spoken well of her? "Margaret wears her circle of friends as a necklace of diamonds." He knew how she could make her friends sparkle, become of greater value to themselves and to everyone by drawing them out, by letting them see that they were capable of living better and nobler lives by "building up the life of thought upon the life of action."

And so after a modest proposal in a letter circulated among the women of Boston, Cambridge, and Concord, Margaret became the presiding genius over a series of Conversations. Twenty-five women came in November 1839 to the first of thirteen weekly sessions, each giving twenty dollars for the series. They gathered in the parlor of Elizabeth Peabody, who, with her sisters, had a lending library of foreign books and magazines in their home on West Street.

Margaret proposed that the group discuss the importance of Greek mythology as their first subject. There were tentative objections from one or two who wondered what significance such study of heathen gods and goddesses could have for modern Christian women. Margaret maintained that "these fables of the gods were the result of the universal sentiments of religion, aspiration, intellectual action of a people whose political and aesthetic life had become immortal; and we must leave off despising if we would begin to learn." She also showed the group how understanding Greek myths was necessary to an understanding of the fine arts—particularly sculpture.

And so the Conversations developed. Margaret opened each discussion, throwing out ideas of her own. Then she welcomed the comments of others. She encouraged the shy ones as well as those more articulate. They blossomed under her guidance.

After one session a member of the group wrote to a distant friend about it:

As I sat there my heart overflowed with joy at the sight of the bright circle . . . I know not where to look for so much character, culture, and so much love of truth and beauty, in any other circle of women and girls . . . Margaret, beautifully dressed, presided with more dignity and grace than I had thought possible. The subject was Beauty. Each had written her definition, and Margaret began with reading her own. This called forth questions, comments and illustrations on all sides . . . The earnestness and simplicity of the discussion . . . gave it the charm of a Platonic dialogue. There was no pretension or pedantry in a word that was said.

There were touches of humor, too, to lighten the high seriousness. But by the end of each session every woman there felt that she had been lifted out of her usually narrow sphere into a larger realm of both mind and spirit.

Margaret continued to hold two series of Conversations each year for the next four or five years, on subjects that ranged from the fine arts to the influence of women on their society. Women who did not attend could not understand the devotion of those who did, and were quick to ridicule the entire project and especially Margaret Fuller, the bluestocking whose influence they distrusted and disapproved of. Why, if they weren't careful, their Miss Fuller would be persuading American women to leave their homes and be like George Sand, that Frenchwoman who wore pants and smoked cigars!

Emerson himself poked gentle fun at what he called Margaret's "Parlortorio." But Margaret knew that he was just teasing, that he really admired her mind and sought her company, although there were times when he was taken aback by her evident self-confidence and by what he called her "mountainous me." However, when it came to selecting an editor for the magazine which he and other Transcendentalists wanted to launch, Margaret was their choice. A woman editor? Unheard of! But Margaret was obviously the most learned woman in the country; she knew everybody worth knowing, and while many people thought her too quick to acknowledge that she found no other intellect equal to her own, others admitted that she might very well be right. At any rate, she and Emerson were enthusiastically named co-editors of the *Dial*, a journal to be published four times a year, one which would spread to a wider audience the new thinking of the Transcendentalists.

It soon became evident that Margaret would do most of the work. She had to coax and cajole and even demand contributions from the men, who seemed ready enough to make speeches but were dilatory when it came to writing articles on time for the printer. When they could not fill up the first issue,

Margaret herself had to write several unsigned articles. But after the *Dial* first appeared in print in July 1840, with its rallying cry for all to join the new spirit of American creativity, there was less difficulty in acquiring material.

The old traditional magazines and newspapers violently criticized the new periodical, radical in its freedom of expression. The Philadelphia *Gazette* called the editors "zanies," "Bedlamites," and "considerably madder than the Mormonites." But such criticisms simply whetted the appetites of the *Dial*'s writers and readers.

Margaret was supposed to be paid two hundred dollars a year for her editorship, but the magazine made little money, so she never did receive that salary. Contributors were not paid at all, but Margaret persuaded some of the best of the New England writers to let her print their offerings: Emerson, of course, and Dr. Channing, with their philosophical essays; Alcott, with his much-too-long "Orphic Sayings"; Henry David Thoreau, with his nature studies; poetry from James Russell Lowell and young Ellery Channing. Margaret herself contributed poems and translations of foreign literature, as well as articles of art and literary criticism. As she began to sign some of her contributions, her name became known in literary circles far beyond the boundaries of

Boston. The *Dial*'s circulation was never large, but it made considerable impact on its readers even in England.

Margaret had to give up her editorship at the end of two years; it was too much of a strain. She suffered from constant and severe headaches. She was paid almost nothing for her countless hours of labor, and she felt that concentrating on her Conversations and on her own writing would be more rewarding.

Her most effective piece of writing for the magazine in 1843 was one to which she gave the cumbersome title "The Great Lawsuit: Man vs. Men, Woman vs. Women." There was nothing cumbersome about the article itself. It was a clear manifesto for women's rights. She wrote: "We would have every path laid open to woman as freely as to man. We would have every barrier thrown down . . . A house is not a home unless it furnish food and fire for mind as well as body." Her article aroused so much interest that later she expanded it into a book, calling it simply *Woman in the Nineteenth Century*. Reaching a much wider audience, the book caused a furor both in America and abroad.

Meanwhile, she was urged to join the experiment in communal living known as Brook Farm. Founded near Boston by her idealistic friends Sophia and George Ripley, it was planned as a utopia—a place where everyone shared work and studies and treated all people as brothers and sisters.

There was much about its high moral purpose that appealed to Margaret. But, like Emerson, she was too much of an individualist to immerse herself for long in communal life. As Brook Farm flourished, Margaret was an occasional visitor, sometimes seeking solitude, sometimes holding informal conversations, and at times joining in the festivities. She was always welcome; one of the cottages was even named for her. But she was never a member of the group, although Hawthorne, later writing his *Blithedale Romance*, led people to think that his heroine, Zenobia, was based on Margaret Fuller's life there.

Family problems continued to occupy much of Margaret's thoughts. Her younger sister, Ellen, more beautiful and more attractive than ever, was engaged to the young poet Ellery Channing. Margaret feared the match; she called it a "family crisis." It was one thing to accept Ellery's gifted poetry for the magazine, quite another to entrust her sister to the uncertain care of an improvident poet—one who had impulsively dropped out of Harvard with no prospects for a career. But they were obviously in love.

Their marriage stirred in Margaret all kinds of tumultuous feelings. She felt apprehension for Ellen and strange pangs for herself. Could they possibly be pangs of envy? She was in her early thirties now. Would she herself never know the joys of marriage? She felt blessed that men like Emerson, her "Waldo," sought her out for her intellect. But would no one court her as a woman? She wrote in her journal: " 'Tis an evil lot to have a man's ambition and a woman's heart."

In 1844, Margaret would have an exciting and unexpected summons from Horace Greeley to New York. He would ask her to become a columnist for his powerful newspaper, the *Tribune*. Perhaps the new life that beckoned would fill both her mind and her heart.

8

ew York was still in the future, however, when in the spring of 1843 Margaret's distant cousin and old friend, James Freeman Clarke, invited her to go on a trip west with him and his sister Sarah. Margaret was eager to go. She had never been west of the Hudson, had never seen Chicago or the lake country or the vast prairies.

Clarke was one of Margaret's intellectual friends, and Sarah Clarke was an artist. Their brother William, who lived in Chicago, would be an expert guide. Margaret knew they would be ideal traveling companions. She could leave her mother in Ellen's care. But there was always the problem of money. Could she afford to go? Sensing the reason for her hesitation, the Clarkes with great tact sent her a check for fifty dollars and a delightful poem that persuaded her to accept.

What an adventure it would be to go west! Chicago was still the Far West to New Englanders, as was the new, raw country beyond, where hundreds of eager families were pouring in by boat, in wagons, or even on foot to settle and begin a new life. Margaret wanted to catch at least a glimpse of this new life. She resolved to keep notes on her travels. Perhaps she could even write a book about her impressions.

In high spirits she set off one bright day in May with James and Sarah Clarke. They stopped first at Niagara Falls and lingered there for several days. The thunder of the waters seemed to envelop Margaret. In contrast to her awe of the great falls was the reaction of another tourist who came up beside her to have his first look. After standing there as though wondering what use he could make of such a sight, he spat into it. Margaret was taken aback. But she decided that this action symbolized the utilitarian view of too many Americans, the mundane approach untouched by the aesthetic or the ideal.

She found this utilitarian view expressed again on the steamboat they took from Buffalo down Lake Erie, Lake Huron, and Lake Michigan to Chicago. She wrote: "The people on the boat were almost all New Englanders seeking their fortune. It grieved me to hear these immigrants . . . talking not of what they should do but of what they should get in the new scene."

To Margaret the new scene was everywhere exhilarating in its strangeness, in the variety of sights and experiences it afforded. She caught her first glimpse of Indians camping on the bank of the St. Clair River.

It was twilight, and their blanketed forms, in listless groups or stealing along the bank, with a lounge and a stride so different in its wildness from the rudeness of the white settlers, gave me the first feeling that I really approached the west.

On meeting William Clarke in Chicago, the small group set out in a huge, lumbering, white-covered wagon to explore the prairies that at first seemed dull to Margaret in their apparent monotony. But the brilliant prairie flowers, the calm sunsets, the feeling that if only she had seven-league boots she could walk forever without meeting any obstacle, soon enchanted her.

She found it equally interesting to stop overnight with the Clarkes at the isolated home of a cultivated Englishman or to put up at a tavern so crowded that she had to sleep on a table in a barroom. She grew deeply concerned with the lot of the women she met —women who had reluctantly left their comfortable old homes, old friends, and familiar scenes to go with their men to this new life. Most of them were unprepared to cope with the hardships and backbreaking toil they encountered.

Margaret hoped that the little girls born in the West would grow up "strong, resolute" and able to enjoy this new rugged life more than their mothers could. But too often the mothers' ambition was to send their daughters back to school in the East. Margaret protested that "methods copied from the education of some English Lady Augusta are as ill suited to the daughter of an Illinois farmer, as satin shoes to climb the Indian mounds."

On the island of Mackinac Margaret visited Indian encampments and wrote with sympathy about the women there, whose wretched condition she deplored. She responded to the freedom of action that the West offered her, and with Indian guides went on an exploring excursion, shooting rapids in a canoe as imperturbably as back in Concord she had stepped into a rowboat with Emerson or Thoreau on placid Walden Pond.

Everywhere she went, everything she saw, everyone she met, aroused her deepest interest. While Sarah Clarke made sketches, Margaret, who did not keep a daily diary, frequently made notes in her Journal, sometimes writing late by candlelight in some crude but hospitable shelter.

On her return to quiet Cambridge, Margaret sorted out her impressions and notes and started writing them up for a book she called *Summer on the Lakes, in 1843.* Finding that she needed to consult reference books and maps, she asked the president of Harvard, Josiah Quincy, and the librarian, John Sibley, if she might study in the college library in Gore Hall. There the best collection of books and maps in the entire United States was housed. A bit startled at Margaret's request, these officials nevertheless gave their permission, recognizing what a serious scholar she was. Thus Margaret Fuller was the first woman ever to penetrate the sacred precincts of the Harvard Library. Absorbed in her work, she paid no attention to the curious and sometimes indignant glances of the undergraduates.

All that winter in the hushed quiet of the academic world she wrote of her enthusiasm for the bustling

*One of the Great Lakes, as it
might have appeared on Margaret Fuller's trip,
engraving by D. Appleton & Company,
New York, 1872*

and turbulent West, her admiration for the Indians, her hopes that settlers would take with them into their new lives a sense of what they could do in their new country rather than just what they could get from it.

According to the custom of her times, Margaret included some irrelevant material: what she had been reading when she was in Milwaukee, even what some of her early school experiences were like, telling the story of the girl she called Mariana. But her pieces concentrating on her summer on the Lakes were fresh, new, and filled with perceptive comment about both places and people.

Her slim book was published in the summer of 1844 by Charles Little and Company (later Little, Brown) of Boston. Margaret was worn out with the writing of it and discouraged when it made almost no impact on an uninterested public. One reader, however, almost made up for the others' indifference. Horace Greeley, dynamic editor of the New York newspaper the *Tribune*, liked it. He liked it so much that he offered Margaret a job on his paper.

He had been hearing about this unusual woman for some time. His wife had attended some of Miss Fuller's Conversations on visits to Boston. When she came back to New York and gave her husband ecstatic accounts of Margaret's intellectual prowess and personal effectiveness, he was at first repelled. A lot of foolishness—this idolatry of a New England bluestocking!

Then he read several issues of the *Dial*. Some of her writing was too rarefied for his taste, but he could not help being impressed by the unprecedented fact that it was a woman who was editor of the magazine. When he read *Summer on the Lakes* he capitulated. Here was a woman who shared his enthusiasm for the West, a woman with ideas, a woman who, when she put her mind to it, could write such a forthright statement as "Wherever the hog comes, the rattlesnake disappears." He asked her to join his staff and write a regular column for his paper.

What a challenge that would be! Margaret was eager to accept. But she was exhausted from the arduous work on her book, and needed weeks of rest. It was agreed that she would not go to the newspaper until late fall or early winter. She recovered her strength when she spent several weeks in early autumn with a friend, Caroline Sturgis, who had a quiet, beautiful place at Fishkill, on the Hudson. The two spent much time rambling out of doors, drinking in the intoxicating colors that they saw all about them.

One rainy day Margaret felt inspired to go to her desk and start writing again. This time she began expanding her *Dial* essay on women's rights into book form. The work went easily and rapidly, and she finished it after she returned to New England, feeling "a delightful glow, as if I had put a good deal of my true life into it."

And so it was that, after completing *Woman in the Nineteenth Century*, Margaret was ready to set out on what she called her "business life."

Most of her friends thought her going to work in New York was too rash a venture. Everyone knew that all intellectual life was centered in Boston! How would a woman with a brilliant and sensitive mind like Margaret Fuller's get along in a brash commercial city like New York? She would soon find out that writing for a popular newspaper and the common multitude was quite a different matter from contributing to the *Dial*, with its small, select subscription list. Margaret could tell that Emerson himself disapproved. For him quiet Concord was the place where his thoughts bore their finest fruit. New York was all right as a stop on a lecture tour, but never a place for the contemplative life that was so essential to the man of thought.

Margaret, full of memories of her recent activities in the bustling West, was unafraid. To "dear Waldo" she wrote somewhat defiantly: "You are intellect; I am life."

Horace Greeley in 1899

The New York Public Library
Picture Collection

Mrs. Fuller wished her daughter godspeed. The two had grown very close during the years that Margaret had put care for her mother first in her life. Now the elderly woman would divide her time among the other grownup and scattered children, paying them long visits. When Margaret left her precious Journals for her mother to keep for her, Mrs. Fuller wrote at the end of the last entry a touching tribute to the love and tender care her daughter had always given her and a prayer to God that he "return her again to me in his good time."

Thus fortified, Margaret arrived in New York, settled in the Greeleys' house at the invitation of Mrs. Greeley, and took up her pen as the first woman member of the working press.

9

*M*argaret found that she was allowed to work either in the Greeley home, called The Farm, or in the city at the newspaper office two miles away. The house was at Turtle Bay, on the shore of the East River opposite Blackwells Island. The spacious frame house recently taken over by the Greeleys was somewhat dilapidated and run by Mrs. Greeley in an absentminded way. It was sparsely furnished, with few touches of elegance; Margaret felt it rather bleak. But she found its setting of eight acres perfectly charming.

A long lane from Harlem Road, where the city omnibus stopped, led past a lively brook and a quiet pond to the house. Going through a wide hallway, Margaret could walk on the long piazza in all kinds of weather, enjoying from there as well as from her bedroom upstairs the sight of boats spreading their sails in the river winds.

She adored "Pickie," the Greeleys' eight-month-old son, and he adored her. She found Mrs. Greeley eager to have their visitor make herself at home. At first Margaret wondered how Horace Greeley, so plebeian, so much a farmer's son, could be such an effective journalist. But as she watched him day after day taking up the cudgels for reform, she grew to admire his courage, his honesty, and his strength. He could write ten columns to her one, and at first he showed his impatience with her more leisurely pace. He drove himself every day, whether he felt well or not, and could not understand Margaret's giving in occasionally to one of her devastating headaches.

But Greeley soon realized what an asset Margaret was to the *Tribune*. At first she concentrated on writing literary criticism, giving praise where she thought it deserved but not holding back unfavorable comment when she thought it warranted. Greeley respected her opinions, realizing that she wrote exactly what she thought of a new book, always telling the truth as she saw it, even though she knew she might make enemies. She dared to write of Longfellow's work, "He has no style of his own." She spoke of his "perpetual borrowing of Imagery." She was even harder on James Russell Lowell's writing, saying, "His verse is stereotyped; his thought sounds no depth, and posterity will not remember him." The genial Longfellow made no reply, but Lowell lashed out at Margaret, making cruel fun of her in his *Fable for Critics*, which was published two years later.

There is one thing she owns in her own single right,
It is native and genuine—namely, her spite;
Though, when acting as censor, she privately blows
A censer of vanity 'neath her own nose.

Margaret Fuller was one of the few to pay tribute to Edgar Allan Poe. In discussing his "The Murders in the Rue Morgue," she wrote: "His narrative proceeds with vigor, his colors are applied with discrimination, and where the effects are fantastic they are not unmeaningly so."

Margaret's own book, *Woman in the Nineteenth Century*, published in New York by Greeley and McElrath in February 1845, brought both cheers and jeers. It was gratifying to her to see her own ideas on woman's role stir up such interest. Margaret wrote home: "It would make you laugh to see mine placarded as 'The Great Book of the Age.'" The whole edition was sold to the booksellers within a week and Margaret received eighty-five dollars as her share of the profits.

The constant theme running through her book was that "inward and outward freedom for Woman as much as for Man shall be acknowledged as a *right*, not yielded as a concession." She held up Mary Wollstonecraft and George Sand as examples of those who, "rich in genius, of most tender sympathies," had broken the narrow bonds put on them by men. In America too, she said, a woman should be educated to her fullest capacities, not just enough to be a better companion to a man. "The fault of marriage and of the present relation between the sexes is that the woman does belong to the man instead of forming a whole with him." She maintained that a woman's love should not be her whole existence.

Margaret knew that men would say, "Now you must be trying to break up the family union, to take my wife away from the cradle and the kitchen hearth to vote at the polls and preach from a pulpit. Of course if she does such things she can not attend to those of her own sphere." Margaret's answer was that "as to her home, she is not likely to leave it any more than she does now for balls, theatres, meetings for promoting missions," and so on.

Margaret repeated what she had written in her essay for the *Dial*: "We would have every path laid open to Woman as freely as to Man."

There was much that was vague and mystical and high-flown in Margaret's book, but there was enough direct challenge to arouse the violent opposition and scorn of many men and even women. Some newspapers called her book hysterical nonsense. But at least one paper called it so important that the editors wished it could be read by every man and woman in America.

Margaret was elated that Horace Greeley reviewed it most favorably in the *Tribune*. Combating injustice wherever he found it, he was of course in agreement with her stand on equal legal and economic rights for women. He had a few reservations, however, feeling that if they wanted equal rights in the business world, women should not expect special treatment in the drawing room.

Remembering her exhilarating visit on a French man-of-war anchored in Narragansett Bay a few years before, Margaret had written of women: "Let them be sea captains if they will!" This produced raucous laughter among the men. And Greeley himself began to tease Margaret by saying he didn't see why he should open a door or pull out a chair for a potential captain of the sea.

But he quite approved of her broadening her sphere of influence. She continued to write of literary matters, of art and music. But she also undertook to visit prisons, talking sympathetically with women prisoners, writing about the sad lot of the prostitutes, crusading in print for a house of refuge for these outcasts on their release. She described the visits to institutions like the Bloomingdale Asylum for the insane, hoping through her column to improve conditions there.

Margaret merely signed her columns with an asterisk. But everyone soon learned whom the asterisk stood for. She became as well known in New York as she had been in Boston. As a celebrity she was invited everywhere, to gatherings of philanthropists and to parties for the literati. But she was often lonely among these strangers. There were many men who admired her, but Margaret knew they paid court to her as an intellectual, not as a woman.

It was at an evening party that she met James Nathan, a blond Jew from Hamburg, Germany. He was ambitious to become a writer but was instead a frustrated businessman. He was attracted to Margaret, who that evening, as always, was the center of attention. Her fine carriage, her elegant dress, her animated conversation drew Nathan to her at once.

On her part she was drawn by this stranger's gentle

mien, his sad blue eyes, his respectful manner, somehow tinged with a kind of audacity.

When he asked if she would go with him to see a diorama of Jerusalem that was then on exhibition in New York, she accepted at once and felt an unaccustomed thrill of anticipation as they settled upon a date to meet again.

The fact that James Nathan was Jewish pleased Margaret, who somehow felt that he must embody the romance of the ancient East, that he must have inherited the awesome power of his Old Testament ancestors. She herself was profoundly religious but felt that in the search for truth and good she should not be bound to any doctrine or creed.

The afternoon they spent together poring over the model of Jerusalem was one of sheer delight. Margaret found her escort not only knowledgeable in the history of his holy city but poetic in his interpretation of its meaning for Jews and Christians alike. More than that, he made it sound as though their viewing the scene together had a very special and personal significance for him. By the time she had to leave to go back to the Greeleys at The Farm, Margaret was sure that the whole afternoon would always hold a special significance for her too.

That night she wrote her new friend a thank-you note that read in part:

Dear Mr. Nathan . . . I have long had a presentiment that I should meet—one of your race, who would show me how the sun of today shines upon the ancient Temple —but I did not expect so gentle and civilized an apparition and with blue eyes!

Then Margaret invited him to attend a concert of Handel's *Messiah* with her. These and other hours they spent together hastened their deepening friendship.

From their first meetings, James Nathan did not treat Margaret like a celebrity; he treated her like a woman. He won her over at once by begging to be allowed to keep the copy of her new book that she had lent him. When he told her about his boyhood and how as a young immigrant to the States he had faced his landlord with tears running down his boyish cheeks, confessing that he had no money, her own cheeks were wet with tears of sympathy for the lad he had been, and one so far from home. He told her his troubles—how now as a man of business he despised spending his days buying and selling, how he longed to travel to romantic places, how he yearned to be a writer. Margaret understood; they were alike in so many ways.

The Greeleys looked with some skepticism upon this new attachment of hers. They obviously did not approve, though Mrs. Greeley was persuaded to allow Nathan to come out when he could to their place in the spring. He took Margaret on walks by the brook, by the pond, and under the blossoming trees.

Spring in that year 1845 was pure magic for her. She had never felt such a complete sharing of nature's beauties as she now did with this dear friend. Together they watched the dogwood turn from palest green to purest white and exclaimed over the budding of the lilac. Later, Nathan braved the thorns of blackberry bushes to pick a bouquet of white blossoms for Margaret, who thought them more beautiful than the most exotic orchids.

They found a secluded spot among the rocks by the river where he sometimes played his guitar and sang German *lieder* to her. Or they had long talks or long silences together.

She did not know just when it was that the miracle had happened. But they both knew it now. She, Margaret, was in love and was loved.

10

*M*argaret and James Nathan saw each other in the greening countryside whenever they could. Sometimes he brought with him his Newfoundland puppy, Josey, who adopted Margaret as his adored mistress.

On most of the days when they had to stay in the city, they stole an hour from their work, meeting on a busy street. They wrote notes or long letters to each other every night and had them delivered by messenger the next day.

Margaret grew less constrained, more confiding

with every missive. "Dear Mr. Nathan" had long ago become "My dear friend," then "My beloved friend," changing to the intimate *"Mein Liebster,"* until finally she addressed him simply as "Dearest."

Things did not always run smoothly between them. Nathan hinted at a mysterious inner bitterness at having been falsely accused of wrongdoing by so-called friends. He implied that he thought it more honorable to keep silent than to protest his innocence. Margaret felt that all should be open and clear between the two of them and she grieved that at first he did not trust her enough to tell her his inmost thoughts.

She called their love a holy love and finally on paper freely expressed her ardent feelings for him. But when he responded at their next meeting with passionate overtures she timidly withdrew, reproaching him for misunderstanding the nature of her emotions. Almost thirty-five years old, she was still too inexperienced in affairs of the heart, too innocent. She was not yet ready to grant to her suitor that a heavenly love might also be an earthly love. She spoke of herself as "a bark that fears to leave the shore."

But misunderstandings that arose were smoothed over for a time. The rapturous letters and meetings continued. Margaret wrote:

Let me sometimes hold you by the hand to linger with me and listen while the grass grows; it does me so much good, the soft warm life close to the earth. Perhaps it is that I was not enough a child at the right time, and am now too childish; but will you not have patience with that?

When once Nathan said to her, "You must be a fool, little girl," Margaret did not take offense. Indeed she was touched; no one had ever said such a thing to her before. She wrote him:

It seemed so whimsical that they [those words] should be addressed to me, who was called on for wisdom and dignity long before my leading strings were off, and so pleasant too. Indeed thou art my dear brother and must ever be good and loving as to a little sister.

But Nathan was not content to play the role of "dear brother" indefinitely. He began to criticize Margaret as too sensitive, a fault she gravely acknowledged. His letters became briefer, less impassioned, his visits to The Farm less frequent. Margaret, who idealized him, made excuses for him. He must not be well, she thought. She herself did not feel well; her headaches grew worse. And she had always thought that a perfect love would bring with it perfect health.

Suddenly Nathan announced that he was going abroad. He felt too confined in his business, he said. He had long wanted to travel. He would go to London, to Rome, to Hamburg to see his mother. He would go to Jerusalem—oh, to so many places.

Margaret was stricken. She listened in silence to his excited plans. What would she do without her dearest friend, her *Liebster?* Yet she who for years had longed to go to Europe herself sympathized with his restless yearnings.

When he finally came to the point of begging her help, she willingly agreed to do everything he asked for and more. Yes, of course she knew he needed money. She would be glad to write her friends in Boston to contribute to a travel fund. Yes, it was a splendid idea that he write and send back articles about his journeyings. Of course she would urge Mr. Greeley to print them in the *Tribune*. And yes, she supposed letters of introduction to important personages in Europe would be helpful. She would write at once to acquaintances who had influential connections in foreign capitals. She would do everything she could to smooth the way for him.

But, oh, how she would miss him! They must spend as much time together as possible these last days. He should come to The Farm whenever he had a few free hours.

Margaret busied herself writing letters on his behalf—requests that she would not have written for herself but that she was happy to make for the man she loved. Her efforts were most successful, and she turned over to Nathan money she had collected and valuable letters of introduction.

Nathan said he was too busy preparing for his departure to come to The Farm to see her more than once or twice. When he did come, Margaret, remembering the intimate, soul-revealing letters she had written him almost daily, begged him to return them all to her so that she might burn them. He said he could not bear to part with them. But he did leave his guitar with her to guard and his puppy, Josey, to care for.

Their parting was painful. At first Nathan said he thought it best for them not to correspond. He wanted to be "unaccompanied" and free to receive new impressions on his journey. But in the end he said he would like to hear from her. And yes, he would answer fully.

Then he was gone!

Margaret began writing to him at once, almost every night adding to a letter that grew longer and longer until at the end of two weeks she could mail it just in time to catch the semimonthly steamer for England. She did this all that summer, addressing the letters to James Nathan in care of a friend of his in London, a Mr. Delf, connected with a publishing house.

Margaret wrote of how she missed him, of how she would steal away to the secluded places where they used to hold their trysts. She wrote of Josey, the dog, who looked at her sadly with questioning eyes at the continued absence of his master. She wrote of young Pickie, the Greeleys' beautiful child, whose devotion was her comfort now. She wrote of her work and how pleased Mr. Greeley was that she had begun giving all her time to the paper. He was even thinking of leaving her in charge when he went on a trip west.

She thought that the seven weeks before she heard anything from Nathan a "cruelly long" time. But she rejoiced to know at last that he was safe and to hear of his activities in England. And yes, she would write to her friend George Bancroft, now Secretary of the Navy, to ask for letters of introduction that the traveler would find useful.

She continued to write unrestrained, warm, and loving letters; she was often disappointed in receiving short, merely friendly letters, some even "cold and scanty"—or, worse, none at all for long periods of time. Then he would send her a token of his love—a book, or a rose from Shelley's grave. And she again would find herself embraced.

To Margaret's pleasure, her mother came to visit her. Emerson came for two days, "full of free talk and in serene beauty, as ever." Marcus and Rebecca Spring, good Quaker friends in New York, carried her off in the heat of the summer to spend time with them in their beautiful country home, Englewood. Their young son Eddie, like all children, adored Margaret and attached himself to her like a small inseparable shadow.

James Nathan sent back his travel pieces and Margaret succeeded in getting them published in the *Tribune.* She thought them well written but sometimes too much like chapters from a guidebook. "Put more of yourself into them," she urged. She did not print the notes on Rome—the Rome she longed to visit—for his descriptions of the sites, the statues, and the buildings there were already too familiar to most readers. She wished he had written instead of life in modern Rome, for she said: "Your observations on what you personally meet are always original and interesting."

Margaret moved into New York for the winter and wrote that she had "an outwardly gay and busy life," meeting new people, making new friends, seeing much of old friends, especially Marcus, Rebecca, and young Eddie Spring.

It was the Springs who urged her to plan to go on a

tour of Europe with them the next August as their guest. They enjoyed playing benevolent hosts to their friends, and Eddie would enjoy everything so much more if Margaret were with them. Margaret was elated at the prospect. But in order to pay at least part of her own way, she and Mr. Greeley agreed that she would continue to write for the *Tribune,* sending back articles whenever she found topics that would interest their readers.

Only one worry kept tugging at the back of her mind. What irony if James Nathan should return to the States just when her lifelong dream of going to Europe at last came true! Surely their angels would not let that happen! Surely he would come to meet her in England. Or she could go to Hamburg if he was there with his family.

Briefly back at The Farm that next spring, Margaret felt a double sadness that the Greeleys were moving to another home, that she herself would be leaving forever the place where she and Nathan had first been in love.

In April 1846 she wrote to him:

This place, I think, will always be lovely in my memory. But alas! We shall meet here no more. Strangers to us will haunt the rocks and little green paths, where we gave one another so much childish happiness, so much sacred joy.

Hast thou forgotten any of these things, hast thou ceased to cherish me, O Israel!

I have felt, these last four days, a desire for you that amounted almost to anguish. You are so interwoven with every thought of this place, it seemed as if I could not leave it till we had walked and talked here once more.

Toward the end of her letter she cried out:

Where are you? What are you doing? I have not heard from you for more than four months. I do not know whether you passed safe through the East, I do not know whether you have ever reached your home. And I do not know what has been or is in your mind. How unnatural! for such ignorance and darkness to follow such close communion, such cold eclipse on so sweet a morning.

In June she received the longed-for answer. He was at last at his home in Hamburg but was exhausted from "excitement of meeting with warm and dear friends after so long an absence and since last Saturday the day of my arrival here dinners, salutations, parties and congratulations did not allow me . . . half enough of necessary sleep." It was only because of his "profound regard and love" for his "dear Margaret" that he was attempting to write now.

In a later letter he wrote at great length the adventures he had had in the East before his return to Hamburg, saying that only lack of a little money had kept him from trying to navigate the Dead Sea. He wanted now to publish a book about his experiences, collecting his newspaper articles and adding to them. He said, "Perhaps you or through your influence can I find a market that may in a measure replenish my bourse."

Referring to Margaret's coming soon to England, he wrote: "You will certainly find something with Mr. Delf in London from me, if not myself, and then thanks to God in all probability shall we meet either here [in Hamburg] or there."

When this letter arrived Margaret was overwhelmed with last-minute things to be done in New York and in Boston, where she was about to pay a farewell visit to her family and friends before sailing on the *Cambria* August 1. But after consulting Greeley about publishing this proposed book she hurriedly wrote Nathan that it might be to his advantage to try to publish in England first. She had collected all his travel pieces from the *Tribune* and would take them with her to Liverpool, sending them to Delf as soon as their ship landed. Delf would know how to proceed from there.

She concluded: "Adieu, may happiness and good be with you. I hope to find a good letter if not yourself in London early in September."

Margaret's hope was based on the promise in Nathan's letter; so why, she wondered, was she assailed by sudden doubts? Could it be possible that neither letter nor *Liebster* would be there to greet her when at last she arrived in the city by the Thames?

11

*I*n spite of disturbing doubts about James Nathan, Margaret was joyful as she went aboard the sailing steamship *Cambria* with the Springs on August 1. The crossing itself was the fastest one ever made between Boston and Liverpool up to that time— only ten days and sixteen hours. But if Margaret had formerly had any idea of wanting to be a sea captain, she now changed her mind. She soon took to her bed in her cabin, seasick and ill from the sound, smell, and jarring vibrations of the engine. Emerging on deck for the last two days of the voyage, she was inspired by the sight of sails set for a favorable wind, making the vessel look like a great winged creature flying across the water. But even more inspiring was her first glimpse of small land birds, the firm shore, and gladsome green fields.

The Springs proved to be ideal traveling companions, as Margaret knew they would be. Like her, they were interested in everything, not only the well-known landmarks that had become shrines for tourists, but the people they met everywhere. They used their letters of introduction to famous figures like Thomas Carlyle, Thomas De Quincey and William Wordsworth, but they also took lively interest in talking to the men and women they encountered on a train, in a stagecoach, on a busy street, or in a country lane. In writing back to the *Tribune*, Margaret followed the advice she had given to James Nathan— not to sound like a guidebook but to make her observations lively, personal, and, wherever possible, significant.

As she had been in New York, she was interested in the opportunities given to workers in the Mechanics' Institutes in both Liverpool and Manchester. Hundreds of men and their families paid a very small fee and eagerly attended evening classes, where they could study everything from mathematics to music.

Margaret was glad to see that girls had recently been admitted to similar classes of their own, where in addition to other subjects, they were taught how to cut out and make their own dresses. She thought all American girls too should learn how to sew.

On the other hand, Margaret was depressed when talking at night in the streets of Manchester "to the girls from the mills who were strolling bareheaded, with coarse, rude and reckless air through the streets, or seeing through the windows of the gin palaces the women seated drinking, too dull to carouse."

The Americans found romantic contrast in traveling by canal boat through a gentle green landscape to the Lake District. In Ambleside they rented a stone cottage and spent a week near an old friend, Miss Harriet Martineau, who, years before, had been the one to arrange Margaret's first visit to Emerson's home. If Miss Martineau was not quite so cordial as they had expected, it was probably because she had not taken kindly to Margaret's criticism of her book ten years earlier when the Englishwoman's *Society in America* was published. There was much about the book that Margaret said she admired, but in her usual forthright manner she had also written to her English friends that she found in Miss Martineau's comments on America a "degree of presumptuousness, irreverence, inaccuracy, and hasty generalization" that was unworthy of the author.

The subject was not brought up between them now that Margaret was a visitor. But Miss Martineau, a great talker herself, had much to say later in her autobiography criticizing what she called Margaret's "incessant harangues." Unfortunately, the two women had become rivals rather than friends.

The travelers had a pleasant visit with seventy-six-year-old William Wordsworth. Even young Eddie enjoyed their call on the revered poet, who took a special interest in the lad as he showed them his modest house and his garden with its rows of hollyhocks. Margaret was disappointed that house and garden seemed tame and suburban as a setting for England's great nature poet.

Margaret found it easy to meet the famous personages of England because she herself had become famous to them through her writings. In Scotland, too, she felt at home, because she was so well acquainted with all the romances of Sir Walter Scott and the ballads of Robert Burns.

She was so enchanted by their stay in the handsome and friendly city of Edinburgh that for hours at a time she gave no thought to their eventual arrival in London, nor did she worry about what word from Nathan might or might not be awaiting her there. And so it was a complete surprise when, just before they left their hotel in Edinburgh for a two-weeks' excursion into the Highlands, she was handed a letter forwarded from London, a letter in the old familiar handwriting.

Her surprise turned to shock when she read the news. James Nathan announced his forthcoming marriage to a young woman in his native Hamburg. The letter went on and on, full of protestations of his great admiration for Margaret, but she scarcely took them in. Admiration she had in plenty from others. It was love that she thought she had from the man who had signed his letters "thy James." How she had been deceived! A sudden headache almost blinded her.

Slowly and deliberately Margaret tore the letter into tiny pieces, discarded them, and in a daze walked out to the stagecoach which was waiting to take them into the Highlands.

There was more bitterness than sorrow in the entry she made in her private Journal that night.

From 1st June, 1845, to 1st September, 1846, a mighty change has taken place, I ween . . . I shall write a sketch of it and turn the whole to account in a literary way, since the affections and ideal hopes are so unproductive. I care not. I am resolved to take such disappointments more lightly than I have. I ought not to regret having thought other of "humans" than they deserve.

That "I care not" was sheer bravado. And she never did write up the experience "in a literary way." Eventually she wrote a correct note of congratulations to "Mr. Nathan" and demanded the return of all her letters. He refused, saying that they had great value to him. He proposed that they could "talk the matter over more fully and fairly" on their return to New York. Margaret got the distinct impression that he had some sort of bargaining in mind. Having no intention of ever seeing him again and being completely disillusioned, she finally concluded their correspondence.

On the trip into the Highlands, Margaret insisted on riding on top of the coach to marvel at the fine views appearing on all sides as the mists lifted. Even one day in a drenching rain she stayed up there enjoying the feeling of solitude and swift flight from old ties and old dreams. Always the sight of hills of purple heather, the sound of the Scottish burr from the people all around her, and the thrilling flourish of the horn announcing every interesting new stop made the trip so absorbing and so memorable that she was almost able to forget her recent humiliation.

She was reminded of it when they went down Loch Lomond in a rowboat toward the inn at Rowardennan, where they would spend several days. As they passed between the bonny banks, the boatman sang a plaintive air about a girl whose lover deserted her, marrying another. Margaret was touched by the sad ballad and by the singer, who obviously was himself moved by the song. Margaret wrote: "I thought this boatman had sympathies which would prevent his tormenting any poor women, and perhaps make someone happy."

But she was finding the mountain air so exhilarating that her headaches disappeared completely and she felt that she could walk for miles and even climb the highest mountain. The opportunity to test her new flow of energy came on the second day of their stay at the inn. It was a perfect day, a rare day for Scotland, clear and bright. Marcus Spring proposed that they see if they could climb Ben Lomond—the highest peak in the area. Rebecca knew it would be too much for her and Eddie, but she urged Margaret to go with Marcus. Other climbers had engaged all the horses, so Margaret and Marcus briskly set out on foot. Because the day was so clear, "one in ten thousand," as the Scots said, they took no guide, although there had been horrendous tales of people, even native shepherds, being lost in the hills in a suddenly enveloping mist.

When they began the actual ascent, they slowed

down and paused every once in a while to admire the views of the lake and the valley below, half hidden between the hills. They climbed for four hours, crossing many small bridges over innumerable springs, finally reaching the peak, where they were rewarded by a most breathtaking panorama. Margaret wrote later that they saw "on every side constellations or groups of hills, exquisitely dressed in the soft purple of the heather, amid which gleam the lakes . . . Peak beyond peak caught from the shifting light all the colors of the prism."

Exulting in their success, the two climbers finally, about four in the afternoon, tore themselves away from the view and began their descent. Soon Margaret felt they had lost the path, because they began to come upon springs that had no bridges over them. Marcus, aware that Margaret was growing tired, agreed that she should rest in that one spot, while he went to find the main path that must be nearby. Soon he did find it and called to Margaret. She followed in the direction where he seemed to be, but she mistook it, overshot it, and could not find him. They kept calling, but the brow of a hill intervened so that they could neither hear nor find each other.

Marcus Spring, deciding that Margaret was finding her own way down, made the long descent to the lake and the inn. Alarmed at discovering that she was not there and did not arrive within an hour or so, he rounded up and sent twenty shepherds with their dogs to search all night for her.

Meanwhile, Margaret kept going to the foot of one hill after another, only to find herself sinking up to her knees in a bog. She could not find a firm crossing anywhere. Once, she threw a stone into the uncertain depths before her. It disappeared so quickly and so completely that she did not dare attempt to go forward there. Again she climbed a hill and sank down utterly exhausted. By now it was dark. Far below she saw a light "about as big as a pin's head." She thought it must be the light from the inn. But she knew she could not make it. Shivering, she pulled her little shawl closer around her, knowing that the safest course was to stay in one spot.

Her feet, her dress, were sopping wet. A cold autumn wind sprang up, the night mists were already falling. She thought she would not live through the night with the fevers and chills that alternately shook her. She kept walking in a small circle to keep her blood circulating. The stars came out briefly, cheering her. But then the mists again surrounded her like visionary shapes; "floating slowly and gracefully, their white robes would unfurl from the great body of mist . . . and come upon me with a kiss pervasively cold as that of death."

Once in a while she would call out as forcibly as she could in case rescuers were near. But she heard no answer. When the moon rose, its light infiltrated the mist, making it silvery. But with the moon's setting, darkness once more surrounded her.

Gradually Margaret felt a peace descend upon her. Later she was to call it a religious experience. Unimportant things, unworthy relationships fell away and only the good and the true remained; they were all that mattered.

At last dawn stole in through the trees, although the mist was still very thick. Margaret started walking again. She drank thankfully from the nearby waterfall and through sheer instinct scrambled in the right direction, calling once in a while until some of the searching shepherds found her. Then her sustaining strength suddenly collapsed and she gratefully let them carry her the long distance to the inn. There was much rejoicing. That night, Margaret wrote in her Journal, "Love Marcus and Rebecca *forever*."

The Springs gave a fine feast in the barn for the valiant shepherds, who in turn put on a lively display of their Highland flings and strathspeys for their hosts. Afterward Margaret asked that they all be brought up to see her in her room, where she was resting and recovering from her adventure. There was such good feeling created between the Scots and the Americans that when the travelers finally set out for Edinburgh and London they felt that they were leaving lifelong friends behind.

12

*O*n their way down from Scotland they stopped at Stratford, where Margaret felt that she was revisiting scenes from her childhood. Here she found the home of Shakespeare, whom she had first discovered on a forbidden Sunday afternoon long ago in her own home in Massachusetts.

Then London, at last! Although they never saw the sun through the fog and coal smoke in the six weeks they were there, Margaret and the Springs found the city an "inexhaustible studio," a world in itself.

When friends warned Margaret that there would be nothing interesting to see or write about in London because Parliament was not in session and the streets would not be thronged with carriages of the rich and fashionable, who were all away because it was not "the season," she laughed. She knew that there would be much for her to write about. Indeed, she was glad that she first saw London without any displays of pomp and circumstance. They would have made the wretched miseries of the poor even more appalling had she seen them in direct contrast.

She wrote to the *Tribune* that squalid misery "stares one in the face in every street of London . . . Poverty in England has terrors of which I never dreamed at home." She expressed concern, too, for the nobles who would have to solve this growing problem of the poverty-stricken. If the aristocracy did nothing to help, they might very well be facing a revolution at the palace gates, as they were in other countries.

Most of the people to whom Margaret had introductions had fled London for sunnier climes. Elizabeth Barrett had just eloped with Robert Browning, leaving London agog at the news. The Brownings were spending their honeymoon in Italy, where Margaret hoped to meet them later.

When Margaret went to the National Gallery and

the British Museum, she found the lighting so poor that she became almost more interested in the people than in the paintings and books. These treasures in the two museums were admired hurriedly every day by nursery maids and groups of workmen who noisily clumped through the corridors in their thick boots on the way home from work. Margaret thought if only they had the leisure to spend a few hours each week in the museums, what an education they could gain.

There were two men in London who came to mean more to Margaret than any others. First of these was Thomas Carlyle, the famous author of *Sartor Resartus* and *The French Revolution*. Emerson had written to this Scottish historian and philosopher a most glowing introduction of Margaret Fuller. "An exotic from New England," he called her.

Carlyle found her a "strange, lilting, lean old maid, not really such a bore as I expected." Margaret was sometimes argumentative, but she was never boring. And the first evening she spent with the Carlyles in the house at No. 5, Great Cheyne Row was a delight; her host was witty and even let Margaret talk now and then and laughed at an amusing anecdote she contributed. Later, in writing to Emerson about the meeting, she said, "Carlyle is worth a thousand of you for that;—he is not ashamed to laugh."

But succeeding evenings were not always so suc-

Thomas Carlyle, 1848

The New York Public Library
Picture Collection

cessful. Once, Margaret blithely declared, "I accept the universe," and Carlyle punctured her balloon by saying dryly, "Gad, you'd better!" At a dinner party given by Carlyle and his wife, Jane, Carlyle's talk turned into a harangue that permitted no interruption. His talk was like a torrent that swept all before him, almost drowning his guests. And if Margaret's head bobbed up for a moment to protest, she was quickly submerged again in the flood of his argument. After dinner when the ladies withdrew into the front parlor, which was papered in a gaily flowered design, Margaret had a conversation with Jane, who until then had not had a chance to say anything. Margaret wrote to Emerson: "I like her very much; —she is full of grace, sweetness, and talent. Her eyes are sad and charming."

Carlyle and Margaret disagreed on how to cure the ills of the world, but they parted with mutual respect. The philosopher wrote to his friend Emerson that Margaret had "a true heroic mind;—altogether unique, so far as I know among the writing women of this generation; rare enough too, God knows, among the Writing Men."

It was at Carlyle's home that Margaret met a man who was to inspire and influence her the rest of her life. This, the second of the two men she most admired in London, was Giuseppe Mazzini, Italian patriot and exile, who could not return to Italy on pain of death. Even in exile he was followed by spies and his letters were opened, but his thoughts were steadfast, fixed on the day when he might lead a successful revolution that would rid his oppressed country of its Austrian overlords and bring about a united Italy, a republic.

Every time she saw him, Margaret listened with rapt attention to Mazzini, who she thought was every bit as heroic as the ancient Romans she had read about when she was a girl. Of course he wore no toga, but his sober black moved her when he explained he was in mourning for his country. He had taken a vow of celibacy when younger, in order to spend all his passionate devotion to his beloved Italia. A slender man with intense dark eyes, short-cropped beard, and mustache, he appealed to Margaret as "by far the most beauteous person I have seen."

She admired the way he had mastered the English language so that he could speak and write eloquently of his plans for his people. She was impressed by his organizing even at a great distance groups of young revolutionaries whom he called "Young Italy." In London, too, he gathered up all the poor Italian youngsters from the streets—the bootblacks, the small peddlers, the beggar boys—and opened an evening school for them.

Mazzini invited Margaret to visit this school and to talk to the pupils on prize-giving night. There she saw ragged boys demonstrate how well they could read and write both English and Italian. And she was delighted to join them at a kind of graduation supper that followed the awarding of prizes. She was touched to see how fervently they admired Mazzini, the man who had rescued them from ignorance and who had given them a new pride in themselves, in their background, and in their hopes for the future.

Because Margaret was steeped in the history of the American Revolution, she was not frightened by the idea of an Italian revolution. Indeed, she wrote back to the *Tribune* to arouse American sympathy for the plight of "suffering nations who are preparing for a similar struggle."

She became even more personally involved when she and the Springs, impressed by Mazzini's spirit of dedication, conspired with him to have him follow them to Paris and then, on a forged passport, join them and enter Rome as a member of their party. Perhaps fortunately for all of them, this dangerous scheme fell through, for Margaret was there in Rome later to welcome Mazzini when he could enter as a Roman citizen and hero.

Paris was next on Margaret's itinerary. There the one person she wanted most to meet was George

Daguerreotype of Giuseppe Mazzini,
taken in Milan in 1848

Istituto Mazziniano

Sand. For a while it seemed impossible. Madame Sand was in the country, living out the half year in seclusion with her family in her château.

Meanwhile, Margaret found that her French was inadequate. She longed to talk in her usual eloquent way with everyone she met. Instead, she found herself balked, frustrated, and reduced to sputtering or silence. She took French lessons every day and began to find herself not only understanding rapid French but being better understood. Her teacher told her she spoke and acted like an Italian, which led Margaret to hope that she would find herself more at home in Italy.

She went to the theater, watching and listening to the great actress Rachel. She reported that in spite of the wretched weather that filled the streets with mud and mist, there was always something interesting to see. She went to the Chamber of Deputies, to lectures at the French Academy, to picture galleries. She even attended a glittering evening and court ball at the Tuileries.

There she witnessed the presentation of the fourteen-year-old Spanish Infanta, Maria Luisa, bride of the Duc de Montpensier, son of King Louis Philippe. From a balcony Margaret saw the girl being taken around the circle of courtiers on the arm of the Queen and thought that the Infanta, "though she looks twenty, has something fresh and engaging and girlish about her." She feared that the artificial life of the court would change that.

Margaret delighted in the fine show, writing later of "the French ladies surpassing all others in the art of dress; indeed it gave me much pleasure to see them. Certainly there are many ugly ones; but they are so well dressed and have such an air of graceful vivacity, that the general effect was of a flower-garden." Margaret noted that several American women present were among the most beautiful, particularly one from Philadelphia who obviously caught the King's eye.

But Margaret was sadly aware that outside the glamour and glitter of court life and of Parisian society were masses of people who were always hungry, who were never warm, who either had no work or were cruelly overworked and underpaid. The winter had been a bitter one. Some religious groups made efforts to help relieve the suffering, but were not able to do enough. Margaret wrote of the need of some radical measures of reform. Here again, as in England, she was conscious of the unrest of the people, the indifference of the upper classes to their plight.

Margaret learned that, in contrast, George Sand, while staying in the country, had given twenty thousand francs of earnings from her novels for the relief of the suffering poor in her province. That was one more reason why Margaret admired this unusual woman and longed to meet her.

When she heard that Madame Sand was finally back in Paris, she wrote her a note at once asking if she might call. The Frenchwoman did not answer. Margaret, soon to leave for Italy, took her courage in her hands and went to the door of Madame Sand's apartment. A maid in picturesque peasant costume answered the bell and went to announce the visitor. She returned to report, "Madame says she does not know you." Margaret felt rebuffed but made one more effort: "Ask her if she has not received a letter from me."

Just then George Sand herself appeared in the doorway and stood looking at her for a moment. As their eyes met, she said simply, *"C'est vous,"* and held out her hand and drew Margaret back into her little study.

Margaret learned that the maid had given the wrong name; the French always had difficulty in pronouncing "Fuller." It had suddenly occurred to George Sand that the caller might possibly be *la dame américaine* who had written her such a charming letter, and so she came to see for herself.

The two women had a long and satisfying talk together—the woman from New England who wrote

George Sand

The New York Public Library
Picture Collection

about woman's freedom and the notorious French-woman who lived her own life of freedom. Margaret had in the past defended George Sand and now she believed more firmly than ever in her essential goodness. She said it was evident in her nature and shone in her eyes. She made a handsome picture in her "robe of dark violet silk, her hair dressed with the greatest taste, her whole appearance and attitude, in its simple and lady like dignity, presenting an almost ludicrous contrast to the vulgar caricature idea of George Sand."

Apparently Margaret impressed George Sand too, for she was persuaded to spend most of the day with her hostess. Thus these two famous and controversial writers became acquainted. No account of this friendship was sent to the *Tribune*, however. Margaret knew only too well how it would shock her readers. She wrote instead to a good friend in Concord who had asked to hear about their meeting. Toward the end of the long letter, she said, "I forgot to mention that, while talking, she *does* smoke all the time her little cigarette. This is now a common practice among ladies abroad, but I believe originated with her."

Later, Margaret met Frédéric Chopin, who lived in the same house in an apartment above George Sand's. "He is always ill," she wrote, "and as frail as a snowdrop, but an exquisite genius. He played to me . . . Madame Sand does not leave him, because he needs her care so much, when sick and suffering."

On her last day in Paris, February 25, 1847, the sun came out, making it the finest day they had had all winter. It shone on the crowds (dressed in their new spring finery) who poured out into the parks and the boulevards. It shone on the little group of Americans, making them almost sad that they were leaving this suddenly beautiful city.

But Margaret was ready for whatever lay ahead. She was impatient now to reach Rome, the city whose sights and citizens she had studied every day throughout her childhood. In Mazzini's latest communication to her he had said: "I would like you to learn to love not only Italy, but the Italians." Margaret was eager to fulfill his wish; it was her wish too.

13

*M*argaret wrote back to the *Tribune*: "There is very little I can write about Italy. Italy is beautiful, worthy to be loved and embraced, not talked about."

She went on: "I have seen all the pomps and shows of Holy Week in the church of St. Peter, and found them less imposing than an habitual acquaintance with the place, with processions of monks and nuns stealing in now and then, or the swell of vespers from some side chapel . . . St. Peter's must be to each one a separate poem."

It was in St. Peter's that Margaret found her own separate poem—one that was to change the rhythm of her life. It was here she met the young Marchese Ossoli.

On Holy Thursday the Springs and Margaret had gone again to see the church at the hour of vespers. After the services they agreed to separate so that they could linger at the various chapels that might interest them most. They arranged to meet later at a certain point in the vast church. Margaret, the puritan from New England, did not subscribe to the Catholic creed, but she walked in solemn reverie, sensing the religious history of the past and the hope of the future inspired by the new liberal Pope Pius IX. She paused at several chapels where candles were being lighted, murmured prayers were being offered, and the devout were kneeling before altars.

Quite suddenly she realized that the time was past for rejoining the Springs. It was growing dark. Hurrying to the place she thought they had agreed upon, she found no one. Nowhere was Marcus to be seen, or Rebecca, or dear Eddie.

At first she waited calmly. Then she became puzzled and, at last, somewhat nervous. She looked about her in bewilderment. Where were her friends?

Quietly and respectfully a young man approached. Might he be of some aid to the signorina? She looked as though she might be lost, he said. He would be glad to be of assistance.

"Grazie," said Margaret, and in her halting Italian she explained her plight.

She could see that the man was younger than she, that he was well dressed, that he was obviously well bred, and that his courtesy was genuine. Together they went looking in one chapel after another. The twilight deepened. It became evident that her American friends, through a misunderstanding, had left the church.

Emerging into the piazza in the dying glow of the Roman sunset, they sought a carriage. But all of the carriages had been taken. None was to be found. There was only one thing to do and Margaret knew it. She gladly accepted the young man's offer to escort her back to her hotel on the Corso.

The conversation during their walk was an odd one. The young man spoke no English but knew a little French. Margaret's Italian was imperfect, to say the least. But with her uncanny ability to draw others out in almost confessional vein, she learned much about this handsome Italian. His name was Giovanni Angelo Ossoli. He was the youngest in an old and titled, but impoverished, family. His mother had died when he was young. He had two sisters and three brothers. Now he, the unmarried one, looked after his ailing father. His three older brothers were in service to the Papacy. One was secretary to the Pope's privy council, and the others were colonels in the Guardia Nobile of the Pope.

And he himself? Margaret asked. Devoutly Catholic of course, he said, but not one to join the Guardia Nobile. His sentiments, he said, with a sudden intense gaze at his companion, were for the new Italy, Italy united, a republic.

Did he follow Mazzini? she asked eagerly—that leader of Young Italy?

"Yes," he said fervently. "And how do you know of Mazzini?"

When Margaret told of her personal friendship with the exiled Mazzini, Ossoli gave her rapt attention. By the time they reached her hotel on the Corso, they felt bound by ties closer than either of them could have imagined one short hour ago.

As they parted, Ossoli kissed her hand with more than the customary Italian gallantry.

Margaret went in to tell the Springs of her interesting encounter and to dream that night of Mazzini saying "Love not only Italy, but also the Italians."

She had heard a great deal about Italian men and how they constantly flattered women with their attentions. It meant nothing beyond the moment, Margaret told herself. She would probably never see this young nobleman again. He had been polite to a stranger, an older woman who could scarcely speak his language. He had kissed her hand on parting, true. But while that might have had some significance in Boston, it meant nothing in Rome. Men were always kissing ladies' hands here. And yet, and yet— Margaret knew that the way Ossoli looked at her, the way he talked to her, the way he responded to Mazzini's name, the way he wished her *Buona sera* as he bade her a lingering good night at the hotel doorway —all of that had to be more than a fleeting flirtation. Perhaps, after all, they would see each other again.

The next day as Margaret stood at her window looking down on the busy Corso, she saw across the street and recognized at once her escort of the day before. Tall and dark, with a luxuriant mustache curling over a sensual mouth, immaculate in the fashionable clothing of the day, twirling a bamboo walking stick, completely composed, unself-conscious, he was gazing upward at the hotel windows as though looking for someone. Margaret's heart began to beat faster. Could he be—he must be—looking for her?

Impulsively she put on her most becoming bonnet, snatched up her gloves and purse, and hurried downstairs. When Ossoli saw her appear at the big, carved front door, he dashed across the street, bowed, and offered Margaret his arm. Off they went to explore together this city that he had grown up in and that she had known well, but only in books and in her dreams.

In the days that followed, Margaret grew to know the city, the language. But more important to her, she grew to know her attentive guide. He was anything but bookish, she learned to her astonishment. His education was limited; he knew only those things that a youngest son of a nobleman had to know in order to live up to the family name. Indeed, he had no career; his main interest now was in caring for his invalid father. He confessed to Margaret that he kept his revolutionary fervor a secret; his family would have disowned him if they had discovered it. It was a joy to him to talk freely to Margaret, who shared with him, as she had with Mazzini, his hopes and dreams for a united Italy.

Those hopes were growing higher every day. When Pope Pius IX granted the populace a sort of representative council, the people went wild with joy. Margaret thought the concession a small one but hoped it would be followed by others. She looked out her window down on the Corso, where the procession of torchbearers flowed past on their way to the Quirinale, the papal palace, to thank the Pope and receive his benediction. She knew that Ossoli was one of them, a part of that river of flame.

Each day he came to guide her, showing her more of his Rome. Each day it became more and more her Rome too. There were feasts and festivals, religious and pagan. There was music in the air constantly, there were flowers blooming everywhere, there was always the sound of church bells, of the clicking of castanets in the streets, where the saltarello was danced by groups of young men and women in the long avenues of ilexes. Everywhere they saw lovers embracing without any self-consciousness. By moonlight in the Coliseum Margaret and her new friend stood close in silent communion, listening to the hooting of those wise birds, the owls.

By now she was his *"cara Margherita."* To her he was her "dear youth," *"caro giovane."* Ancient Rome became new as they saw it through each other's eyes and as they felt it casting its spell over both of them.

But through all of this enchantment there was in both of them the constant awareness that the deepest needs of the people would not be met as long as Italy remained divided and under foreign domination. The Pope was not ready to make any drastic reforms.

All printed matter was censored. And even if it hadn't been, barely 10 percent of the population could read. To Margaret, whose great cure for the poverty-stricken of the world was education, this was an intolerable situation. Remembering Mazzini's

Marchese Ossoli

By permission of the Houghton Library,
Harvard University

night schools for beggar boys in London, she longed for the revolution in Italy that would bring such benefits to the people here. Beneath the music and the dancing and within the sound of all the church bells, there was vast ignorance, real oppression.

When Margaret's stay in Rome was drawing to a close and she was scheduled to leave with the Springs in another week, Ossoli was desolate. He vowed he had never known anyone who meant so much to him as his Margherita. In despair at the thought of losing her, he proposed marriage.

Margaret was stunned. She was already more than half in love with Ossoli. If she allowed herself she could be deeply in love with him, but she knew only too well what it would cost him to marry her—a woman who was poor, a Protestant, American, in uncertain health, and ten years older than he. Worst of all, she would be considered a radical. He would be disinherited by his family and perhaps even cast off by his church. No; she couldn't possibly marry him. In every way it was unsuitable.

If she were George Sand, she thought to herself, she would follow her impulses and yield to his love even without marriage. But she was not George Sand, she was Margaret Fuller, puritan from New England. Her pride buoyed her up as she said goodbye to Ossoli. But she almost broke down when he embraced her in farewell; then he looked at her with pleading eyes and said hopefully and even with a touch of assurance, "You will return to me."

She went with the Springs to Florence, finding it rich in art and new acquaintances. Margaret had an introduction to the Marchesa Costanza Arconati Visconti, of one of the finest of Italian noble families. The Marchesa and her husband had been allowed to return to Italy after years of exile—an exile forced upon them by the Austrians because of their activities on behalf of an independent Italy. They found in Margaret a sympathetic and intelligent ally. She found in the Marchesa the kind of "really high-bred lady" she had not met before. The Marchesa treated her like a sister, introducing all of her titled friends. Margaret enjoyed their hospitality but could not help thinking of the irony of her being received so warmly by these strangers, whereas in Rome her much deeper friendship with the Marchese Ossoli had to be kept secret from his titled family and their circle, whose ideas of politics and patriotism differed so from his own and from hers.

Margaret dutifully wrote to the *Tribune* about Florence and about her future travels. But in Venice she bade an affectionate farewell to the kindly Springs, who were leaving to go to Germany. She told them that she had little or no interest in Germany.

She would stay for a while in Venice, then travel by herself in northern Italy. She told them that she could not bear to leave Italy before she had learned to know it better. She did not tell them that what she really could not bear was the thought of leaving Rome forever—Rome and Ossoli.

14

*I*t was not until the autumn that Margaret returned to Rome. She had found both advantages and disadvantages in traveling by herself. She could go when and where she pleased, but she missed her American companions and she missed Marcus Spring's quietly efficient touch in making arrangements for transportation and lodgings.

She became ill at Brescia. Suffering chills and fever, she had a bed made in a carriage so that she might be driven to Milan. There she recovered to find revolutionary spirit running high against Austrian rule. She escaped the hot weather at Lake Maggiore and at Bellagio. In Florence she was ill again and was rescued and cared for by an American sculptor, Joseph Mozier, and his wife. It was not until she was in Rome in mid-October that she completely recovered.

She wrote to Marcus Spring: "All mean things were forgotten in the joy that rushed over me like a flood. Now I saw the true Rome . . . All other places faded away, now that I again saw St. Peter's, and heard the music of the fountains."

What Margaret heard too was the music of Ossoli's renewed avowals of love. This time his passionate pleas swept away all lingering restraints. She did not think of George Sand; she no longer thought of the puritan Miss Fuller from New England. She thought only of herself as Margherita in Rome, and Ossoli, who had become her *"caro Angelo."*

That autumn of 1847 was a glorious one for the lovers. They united their two passions—for each other and for a new Italy. Margaret settled into lodgings on the Corso near the Piazza del Popolo, where she could look out and see all that was going on in Rome. Here Ossoli could visit her every day. Here she could study and write her *Tribune* columns, which were becoming more and more political. Here she began thinking of writing an important book, a firsthand account of the growing ferment in Italy. Here on Monday evenings she was "at home" to other Americans who had grown fond of her and wanted to discuss the changing Italian situation. Among these were William Wetmore Story and his wife, Emelyn. Story was a lawyer who had left the law and Boston behind him to enjoy the artist's life in Rome and to work seriously at becoming a sculptor.

The Storys marveled at the changes that had come over Margaret. Remembering her in Cambridge as one "on intellectual stilts, with a large share of arrogance, and little sweetness of temper," they were delighted to see how she now radiated happiness and was simple and affectionate with them all. At first they did not guess that the cause of this transformation was the young Marchese Ossoli, whom they met frequently in Margaret's little salon. He impressed them as reserved and gentle, a quiet guest who sometimes slipped out when the English-language conversations became too much for him.

Margaret had indeed changed. In mid-December she wrote her mother: "My life in Rome is thus far all I hoped. I have not been so well since I was a child, nor so happy ever, as during the last six weeks."

Once, long ago, Margaret had written in her private Journal how she longed someday to have a child.

She wrote then: "I have no child of my own, and the woman in me so craves this experience it seems the want of it must paralyze me."

Now, in December, she learned that she was to have a child—hers and Ossoli's. But she had never dreamed of becoming a mother without first being a wife. Instead of being filled with joy, she was filled with dismay. Her puritan conscience was once more aroused. Ossoli was tenderly solicitous. He would never leave her, he said, and Margaret knew it was true. But if the idea of marriage before had been difficult, now it seemed impossible. Ossoli's father, who might have arranged for a special dispensation for his son's marriage to a Protestant, had died. The three older brothers were holding on to the inheritance. They were hostile to the young Angelo because by now he had openly allied himself with the people, joining as a volunteer the newly established Guardia Civile, the Civil Guard. The oldest brother had forced him out of his quarters in the upper floors of the family palazzo. He moved into the first-floor apartments with his married sister, who was sympathetic but powerless to help him in any other way.

He was almost penniless. He wanted desperately to marry his Margherita but did not see how that could be done at present. They could not be married in the church, and civil marriages were not permitted anywhere in Rome. All they could do now was to wait and hope for the uprising of the people in Rome which, if successful, would remove all obstacles. The young Ossoli would hold an honorable place in the people's new government; then he could marry either in the church or out of it. He could demand his share of what his father had left his sons. But whatever happened, he promised, he would welcome his child and give him his name, and they could bring him up in the freedom of the new Italy. Meanwhile, he concluded sadly, it would be best to keep all secret.

Margaret agreed and prayed that all might go well with them, but she found it difficult to see much hope in the future. She, too, was almost penniless. The money from her articles—never very much—would diminish as the months wore on and as she would be able to write less and less. At home her rich uncle had died—the one who had been a grudging guardian to the Fuller children after their father's death, who so disapproved of Margaret's spending money on her brothers' and her sister's education. For a while she hoped for a large bequest from him, but she soon learned that his small fortune was to be divided among more than sixty heirs. Margaret's share would be a pittance. To whom could she turn? Not to her dear family, who she was sure would never be able to understand her plight. Not to any friend either here or at home. The Springs were far away; the friendly Storys had left for the winter.

All was discouraging, even the weather. After the glorious autumn came the dreary winter. It rained, it poured every day, a cold rain that permeated the unheated stone buildings and chilled Margaret to the bone. She wrote: "The ruins and other great objects appear terribly gloomy, steeped in black rain and cloud; and my apartment . . . is dark all day."

Margaret felt she could not confide completely in anyone. In the new year she did write to her friend Caroline Sturgis in sad foreboding:

I have known some happy hours, but they all lead to sorrow . . . When I arrived in Rome, I was at first intoxicated to be here . . . That is all over now, and with this year I enter upon a sphere of my destiny so difficult that at present I see no way out except through the gate of death. It is useless to write of it. You are at a distance and cannot help me . . . I have no reason to hope I shall not reap what I have sown, and do not. Yet how I shall endure it I can not guess; it is all a dark, sad enigma.

In spite of encouraging rumors of uprisings in various other parts of Italy, and in spite of her desperate need to make money, Margaret hadn't the strength to write much to the *Tribune* during the first months of her pregnancy. She had constant nervous headaches and was weakened by the chills and fever that plagued her and by her inability to eat anything except rice and the vegetables that were difficult to find in the winter—all except the "horrible cabbage," which seemed always available.

Ossoli's loyalty and love were all that sustained her during this desolate period. Then, toward the end of March, the rains ceased, the Italian skies were once again their deep blue. Margaret's health revived and her spirits rose with the singing of the larks that winged their way above the Roman ruins.

From Milan, from Venice, and from most of northern Italy, as well as from Sicily and Naples, news of successful uprisings came to Rome. Margaret rejoiced with the people and wrote:

With indescribable rapture these tidings were received in Rome. Men were seen dancing, women weeping with joy along the street. The youth rushed to enroll themselves in regiments to go to the frontier.

Margaret wrote to a friend in America:

I have been engrossed, stunned almost, by the public events that have succeeded one another with such rapidity and grandeur. It is a time such as I always dreamed of . . .

I rejoice to be in Europe at this time and shall return possessed of a great history . . . At present I know not where to go, what to do. War is everywhere . . . the men of Rome are marching every day into Lombardy.

She received letters from her family, from Emerson, from others, all urging her to return to the safety of her home in America. Eugene, her favorite brother, was happily married and wanted her to meet his bride. Brother Richard said he would never marry and urged her to come live with him. Ellen and her poet husband were unhappy together; she needed her sister. Her mother was worried about her. Emerson wrote from London: "You are imprudent to stay there any longer. Can you not safely take the first steamer to Marseilles, come to Paris, and go home with me?"

She could not explain to anyone, certainly not to her "dear Waldo," why she could not go home at this time. She said that she was collecting documents so that she could write and be "possessed by a great history" when she should return. But it was her personal history that possessed her now.

With Ossoli, her *"caro Angelo,"* she had to plan and to plot where she could go to have her child in safety and in secrecy. First they chose Aquila, a town high in the Apennines, as her shelter—far from the curious eyes of fellow Americans and Romans. But after Margaret lived there a few months, it seemed too isolated, too far from Ossoli, who could not come to see her often enough. He was now not only on volunteer duty with the Civil Guard in Rome but he had acquired a poorly paid part-time job in the office of an uncle; it had something to do with administering an estate. When Aquila was occupied by soldiers who disarmed and imprisoned some of the local guard, Margaret decided to move to Rieti and have her baby there.

Rieti was just a day's or night's ride in the diligence from Rome, and now it was easier for Ossoli to come to spend time with her. Between visits they wrote to each other by every post, and because they suspected their letters were read by the censor, they were careful as to how they spoke of political affairs. Indeed, Margaret was hungry to receive his letters of love, which she answered with equal ardor. These letters of hers were far different from the high-flown, rarefied missives she had once written to the unresponsive Nathan.

These were almost wifely letters—filled with longing for her absent loved one, but also filled with anxious thoughts about her dwindling supply of money, fears of her coming ordeal, only a few weeks away now, but also with hope that her *"caro amico"* would be by her side during the birth of their child. When she learned that Ossoli might be called up with the guard any day to go to the frontier to defend Bologna against the invading Austrians, she was in despair. But she wrote as calmly as possible to the agitated Ossoli, who was beside himself in his struggle between love of country and love for Margaret in this double crisis.

Since Bologna was within the papal domain, most Romans expected the Pope to send the Civic Guard at once to defend that city. At first the Pope said he wanted them all to go. Then he vacillated and delayed giving the final order, revealing once more his timidity in temporal affairs.

Margaret's time was almost upon her. She wrote Ossoli:

If I were sure of being all right, I would want very much to pass through this trial before your arrival. But— when I think I could die alone, without being able to touch a dear hand . . .

No wonder she was fearful. Here she was, a woman thirty-eight years old, far from family and friends who didn't even know of her plight, a foreigner in a strange city where medical practice was primitive, depending on a simple midwife to help in her crucial hour, with no husband but a lover who might not even be able to come when she desperately needed him.

But Ossoli did come the following weekend. He was able to soothe and sustain his Margherita in her prolonged labor. The midwife was there for the difficult delivery. And both mother and father, on Tuesday, September 5, 1848, welcomed their baby son, who was scarcely as long as his name—Angelo Eugenio Filippo Ossoli.

15

For a time all troubles were forgotten in Margaret's rapture in holding her son. It took her a long time to recover from his birth, and she was disappointed that she was unable to nurse him and needed to engage a wet nurse. But she exulted in her motherhood and wrote notes to Ossoli about her treasure.

He is very pretty . . . and all the people around call him Angiolino [*little angel*] *because he is so lovely. He has your mouth, hands, feet. It seems to me that his eyes will be blue. For the rest, he is altogether a* birbone [*rascal*], *understands well, is very obstinate to have his will.*

Again she wrote Ossoli: "He is always so charming, how can I ever leave him? Awake in the night, I look at him, think, ah! it is impossible to leave him."

This was in October, when they began to discuss when Margaret would be strong enough to go back to Rome to be near Ossoli and resume writing for the *Tribune.* She agreed that until they could be legally married, the baby should be left with the nurse in Rieti.

Meanwhile, a frightening epidemic of smallpox broke out in the village. Margaret implored the local doctor to come and inoculate the child. He delayed and kept on delaying. Margaret was frantic with worry and did not dare take the baby out any more. For a while she had thought it safe to walk in the bishop's garden, but another child had died of smallpox there. No place was free of danger. Finally the doctor confessed he had no vaccine. Margaret wrote Angelo at once, begging him to find and send a supply of vaccine from Rome immediately. This he did, and the local doctor inoculated little Angelino.

Ossoli insisted that the baby be baptized and be given his name. This was difficult to arrange but was finally done on November 6. Along with the baptismal certificate, Ossoli and the priest signed another document proclaiming in Latin that the infant was his son and would inherit the title Marchese and all other rights and privileges of the Ossoli name.

Now all was in readiness for Margaret to leave her child and return to the world of politics and revolution, from which she had been absent for longer than five months. But she and Ossoli had to postpone their departure for Rome several days because of torrential rainstorms that flooded the rivers and overflowed the banks and bridges. Travel was still very risky when they finally set out in the diligence. Margaret wrote later to her mother that in the moonlight, "as we approached the Tiber, the towers and domes of Rome could be seen, like a cloud lying low on the horizon. The road and the meadows, alike under water, lay between us and it, one sheet of silver. The horses entered; they behaved nobly; we proceeded, every moment uncertain if the water would not become deep; but the scene was beautiful, and I enjoyed it highly. I have never yet felt afraid when really in the presence of danger, though sometimes in its apprehension."

For many months to come Margaret was to be "really in the presence of danger." Her new lodging consisted of one large room only, but it was sunny, it was cheap, and best of all it looked out on the Piazza

Barberini, where she could watch what went on at that palace and at the Pope's.

What went on was an amazing series of fearful events. On November 15, Rossi, the much-hated minister of the Pope, was assassinated. All of the people and most of the soldiers rejoiced to be rid of one they knew to be a tyrant. Next, when the troops and the people together went to the Quirinale to demand less oppressive measures, the Pope refused to appear before them. When the people attempted to force the door of the Pope's palace, the Swiss Guard fired into the crowd. The Pope's Latin Secretary also fired from a window. Margaret looked down from her window to see the wounded carried away on stretchers.

The Pope had not ordered these cowardly acts, but he did not condemn them. The people who adored him as their spiritual leader were now denouncing him as their temporal leader. The Church should no longer be their state! The Civil Guard, Ossoli among them, were protecting the Papal Palace. The Pope was still afraid to appear. For days he remained behind locked doors until the evening of the twenty-fourth, when, disguised as a simple priest, he made his escape in the carriage of the Bavarian minister and was driven to the territory of the Bourbon King of Naples, where he took refuge in the fortress of Gaeta.

His unnecessary flight seemed to the people an abdication and a betrayal of all their hopes. Margaret wrote about the situation in such strong terms that church officials in America protested her articles. Greeley, however, printed them just as she sent them in.

In part she said about the Pope:

> *There can be no doubt that all his natural impulses are generous and kind, and in a more private station he would have died beloved and honored; but to this he was unequal; he has suffered bad men to surround him, and by their misrepresentations and insidious suggestions at last entirely to cloud his mind.*

She went on to protest bitterly his flight to the enemy in Naples, throwing himself "in the arms of the bombarding monarch, blessing him and thanking his soldiery for preserving that part of Italy from anarchy!"

To Margaret the protest of the people in Rome was far from anarchy. It was merely their way of demanding simple justice. She went on:

> *In a few days all began to say: "Well, who would have thought it? The Pope, the Cardinals, the Princes are gone, and Rome is perfectly tranquil,*

*and one does not miss anything except that there are
not so many rich carriages and livery."*

Margaret urged America to side with the people
and in the future to

*send here a good Ambassador—one that has ex-
perience of foreign life, that he may act with good
judgment. And send a man capable of prizing living
in, or knowing Rome; the office of Ambassador is
one that should not be thrown away on a person who
can not prize or use it.*

Did she suddenly realize she was describing herself? She must have realized this, because she added:
"Another century, and I might ask to be made Ambassador myself . . . but woman's day has not come
yet."

The beginning of that winter, so different from the
bleak, rainy months of the year before, was full of
activity for Margaret. She spent Christmas week in
Rieti with her baby son, writing to Ossoli, who was
on guard duty, that she would have a thousand things
to tell him about their Angelino.

Back in Rome she again turned from private plea-
sures to public events, which, peaceful at first, rapidly
accelerated into open warfare. Margaret, always writ-

ing with passion for a united Italy, used her pen as one weapon in the defense of Rome against her enemies.

She had in January recounted the scorn of the people when they received word from the absent Pope that "all who took part in that 'detestable' act of constitutional assembly would be excommunicated." To most Romans and Margaret, electing the National Assembly had been the grand democratic gesture of the people. They sent envoys to the Pope, but he refused to receive them. Now it became clear that Pope Pius IX would not acknowledge the people's government. Indeed, he appealed to heads of state in Austria, Spain, and France, and even to the President of the United States for help to preserve his temporal power.

To Rome's new government as deputy came one of Italy's heroes, Garibaldi, wearing his black, broad-brimmed hat with its ostrich feather and his long red tunic. At first Margaret looked upon him with some distrust. Unlike her hero Mazzini, he commanded a guerrilla band of warriors. This time he had left them behind in Rieti. She hoped Angelino would be safe in any disorders that might arise there.

On February 9 the republic was proclaimed, and Margaret wrote up the great event. A few days later, to Margaret's joy, Mazzini was sent an official invita-

tion to return with full Roman citizenship and to become a member of the assembly. Posters went up all
over Rome to welcome home their exiled hero. In his
first address to the assembly he inspired them all with
his ringing phrases: "After the Rome of the Em-
perors, after the Rome of the Popes, will come the
Rome of the People."

It was only a few nights later that Margaret, while
Ossoli was with her, answered the door to find her
friend Mazzini standing there, eager to talk. They did
talk, the three of them, exchanging views and news of
reforms planned by the assembly and of foes both inside and outside Rome that were already threatening
the new republic. Margaret felt that if anyone could
save Rome it would be Mazzini. But clearly a crisis
was at hand and even Mazzini was pessimistic.

In only three weeks Rome found herself surrounded. To the south were the armies of the Bourbon King of Naples. To the north and east were the
armies of the Austrian Emperor. To the west at sea
were the ships of Spain. Most threatening of all, the
French under President Louis Napoleon were sending an expeditionary force under General Nicolas
Oudinot, the son of one of Napoleon's top generals,
to Italy, ostensibly to aid the Romans but actually to
restore the Pope and advance French power against
the Austrians.

When Oudinot's aide, Colonel Leblanc, came to Mazzini and reported that the French wished only to protect the Romans from the Neapolitan and Austrian armies and to restore the Pope to his people, Mazzini asked, "And if the people do not want the Pope restored, what then?" The answer was, "He will be restored, just the same."

The assembly then knew the true nature of the French "protection" and voted unanimously not to welcome them but instead to resist. By the time the French fleet arrived with its armies in the port only forty miles northwest, the people were frantically throwing up earth mounds and barricades around the city, preparing to meet force with force.

Margaret, going to see these warlike preparations with Emelyn and William Story, who had returned to Rome, knew then that the time for talk had passed. The time for action had come.

Her own call to action came on April 30, when a messenger appeared at her door with this note:

Dear Miss Fuller,

You are named Regolatrice of the Hospital of the Fate Bene Fratelli. Go there at twelve if the alarm bell does not ring before. When you arrive there you will receive all the women coming for the wounded and give them your

directions so that you are sure to have a certain number
of them, night and day. May God help us.

It was signed, Cristina Trivulzio di Belgioioso. She
was known in Italy as the "Revolutionary Princess," a
beautiful and wealthy partisan of the people. She had
met Margaret and counted on her as a reliable and
loyal aid.

The note filled Margaret with fear for Ossoli. She
knew that as a sergeant in the Guard he would be in
the thick of forthcoming battles. But the note also
gave her a sense of exultation, for now she would
have the opportunity to act. Now at last she would
put aside the pen and take up her post as director of
nurses at one of the hospitals, where she could be of
great help to the men defending Rome. Thank
heaven her darling Angelino was still up in Rieti,
away from immediate danger.

Already the wounded were being brought in from
skirmishes outside the walls of the city. Later, Margaret wrote:

The night of the 30th of April I passed in the hospital,
and saw the terrible agonies of those dying or who needed
amputation, felt their mental pains and longing for the
loved ones—many were students of the University, who

had enlisted and thrown themselves into the front of the engagement.

Garibaldi was able to repulse the first attacks of the French. But in the weeks that followed, Margaret, constantly at the hospital, learned at first hand the bitterness of almost certain defeat. When after a fake truce and a few incredibly brave and successful sorties by Garibaldi the French began to bombard the city, she lived in daily terror that Ossoli would be one of the wounded and dying brought in to the hospital on stretchers. So far he had escaped injury, but he was stationed in one of the most dangerous posts—on the walls by the Vatican. He fought so tirelessly and bravely that he was promoted to a captaincy. Sometimes in a lull of the fighting Margaret went to him, taking a basket of provisions and having a poignant and all-too-brief talk with her beloved soldier.

At times, in the midst of the cannonading, her own life was in such danger that she finally decided she must confide in her good friend Emelyn Story. She told this sympathetic woman of the existence of her baby in Rieti and gave into her keeping certain documents, including those of the child's baptism and inheritance. She begged her, in the event of Margaret's and Ossoli's deaths, to take little Angelino to America, delivering him safely to Mrs. Fuller, her mother, along with a long letter of belated explanation which Margaret prayed her mother would accept with love and understanding.

Emelyn Story looked at her friend, so troubled and exhausted but still so loving and courageous, and promised to do everything that she was asked. She did not even tell her husband of Margaret's confidence, nor did she read any of the letters entrusted to her. Later, before the Storys left the city under a white flag, taking refuge in Germany from the siege, she returned into Margaret's keeping the packet of documents and letters unopened, but repeated her promise to take Angelino to America if Ossoli and Margaret did not survive.

Now in the last days of the fierce bombardment that was devastating her beloved city and killing many brave Italians, including Ossoli's comrades, Margaret was one of the few foreigners left in Rome. Lewis Cass, Jr., the American envoy, was another. He had become acquainted with Margaret and admired enormously her courage and the way she stuck to her perilous post in the hospital, where she worked valiantly to give aid and comfort to the wounded until the end.

The end came on July 4 when the victorious French entered the city. Margaret looked down on them from her window, bitter and desolate. Ossoli could not bear to look. He sat inside, weeping. It was the end of all their hopes for Italy and for themselves.

Garibaldi had defiantly moved into the hills with his men, hoping to continue a fight that was really hopeless. Mazzini, under an American passport obtained for him by Margaret, went once more into exile.

Under French occupation, Rome was put under martial law, the Guard was stripped of its few remaining arms, and a proclamation was issued that all foreigners who had aided the republic must leave Rome within twenty-four hours or face imprisonment or death. Lewis Cass succeeded in getting horses and a carriage for Ossoli and Margaret, whose only hope now was to be reunited with their child in Rieti.

They found him worn to a skeleton, having been fed for months only on bits of bread soaked in wine. He was so near death that Margaret wrote to Lewis Cass that "if he dies, I hope I shall, too. I was too fatigued before, and this last shipwreck of hopes would be more than I could bear."

16

*M*argaret and Ossoli tended to and hovered over their child day and night until with inexpressible relief they saw him manage his first wan smile and lift his small hand to touch their loving faces. Now they were a family, so closely bound to one another that nothing could ever separate them.

Marriage had long been postponed so that with the triumph of the republic they might gain honorable recognition from Ossoli's family and win his rightful inheritance. Now all hope for both recognition and patrimony had been lost in the lost hopes for the republic. So sometime, somewhere, no one knows exactly when or where, at Ossoli's insistence and with Margaret's consent, the marriage ceremony was privately performed and Margaret finally became legally not only a wife but a marchesa.

Margaret wrote to her friend the Marchesa Arconati Visconti of her marriage:

> *It seems to me silly for a radical like me to be carrying a title; and yet, while Ossoli is in his native land it seems disjoining myself from him not to have it . . . to drop an inherited title would be, in some sort, to acquiesce in his brothers' disclaiming him, and dropping a right he may wish to maintain for his child.*

But to Margaret the most important and the most difficult letter she wrote about her new family was to her mother. Here she was, herself mother of a child almost a year old—a child whose existence and whose father's existence were completely unknown to Mrs. Fuller. Remembering New Englanders' strict standards of morality and their reaction to any hint of scandal, Margaret feared more than anything else for her mother's peace of mind. Fortunately her genuine love for her mother helped her to write from the heart.

In part she wrote:

The first moment, it may cause you a pang to know that your eldest child might long ago have been addressed by another name than yours, and has a little son a year old.

But beloved mother, do not feel this long. I do assure you that it was only great love for you that kept me silent. I have abstained a hundred times when your sympathy, your counsel, would have been most precious, from a wish not to harass you with anxiety. Even now I would abstain, but it has become necessary, on account of the child, for us to live publicly and permanently together.

Margaret then described her husband as a member of a noble but impoverished family. She admitted that he was not an intellectual but wrote of his unswerving love for her. She confessed that he was younger but that so far it had made no difference. "However my other friends may feel, I am sure that you will love him very much and that he will love you no less."

Then, following a glowing account of their son, she added: "Write the name of my child in your Bible, Angelo Ossoli, born September 5, 1848. God grant he may live to see you and may prove worthy of your love!"

When Margaret received her mother's reply, she was so relieved that she felt like Christian in *The Pilgrim's Progress* when the great burden finally rolled off his back. Of course her mother had been startled by her daughter's news. But after reading and rereading the letter from Italy, after carefully considering the situation, Mrs. Fuller wrote without reserve. She said of Ossoli:

If he continues to make you happy, he will be very dear to me . . . I send my first kiss with my fervent blessing to my grandson. I hope your husband will understand a little of my English, for I am too old to speak Italian fluently enough to make him understand how dearly I shall love him if he brings you safe to me.

Now in September the little family moved to Florence, where Margaret settled down to write her history of the rise and fall of the Roman republic. When they had hurriedly left Rome, Margaret was careful to bring all her notes with her: her journals, newspaper clippings, letters from Mazzini, the Pope's proclamations, the pronouncements of the General Assembly—all the documents that had bearing on the great struggle. All of these, when added to her own and Ossoli's personal experiences and recollections, were surely the raw material from which one of the great eyewitness accounts of the revolution could be written. Margaret knew that and was resolved to write a history that would present to the world the true account of the lost cause. It would be her masterpiece.

It would also have to be their living. They had barely enough money to see them through the winter. Without explanation Greeley had dropped her as correspondent for the *Tribune*. Now that her secret marriage had become known at home, Margaret wondered if Greeley had been dismayed by the gossip about her that must be going the rounds in Boston and New York. She could almost hear the questions, the speculations, the insinuations that would be exchanged across teacups and dinner tables at home. "What! Margaret Fuller suddenly appearing with a year-old child and a husband that no one has ever heard of! He claims to be of the nobility, imagine! And she is to be addressed as the Marchesa Something-or-Other!"

Thank heaven, her mother and those friends who really mattered remained loyal. In Florence also, the American-English colony was at first taken aback by Margaret's appearance with an unknown husband and child. Elizabeth Barrett Browning was one of those who looked upon her at first with doubting curiosity. But with dignity and her usual personal

Robert Browning

The New York Public Library
Picture Collection

Elizabeth Barrett Browning,
engraving by J. C. Buttre, New York

The New York Public Library
Picture Collection

magnetism Margaret made friends of the Brownings, and was soon welcomed into the small circle of writers and artists.

She wrote steadily on her History but saved part of each day for playing with her child and taking walks with him and Ossoli. They could not afford a horse and carriage. Indeed, they could afford very little outside the daily essentials. As their supply of money dwindled and as the History grew and as the winter gave way to early spring, Margaret thought long and hard about returning to America. It seemed the only way now for her to sell her manuscript and have her book published, and so earn their daily bread. True, Ossoli was not equipped in any way to work at anything in the States, but it was also true that there was no longer any opportunity for him in Italy. Indeed, the Austrian police in Florence were looking upon this republican exile and his foreign wife with increased suspicion. Margaret and he both were uncomfortable under their constant surveillance, fearing that they might be asked to leave Florence. Lewis Cass wrote that the situation in Rome was frightful; it would not be possible for them to go back there. Little Angelino was the one carefree spirit among them as he joyfully clapped his hands in time to the beating drums and the passing parades of soldiers in the streets of Florence.

Once Margaret had made up her mind that she could support her little family and have a better chance of keeping them safe and happy in America, she started looking for the best but cheapest passage available to them. She was apprehensive about the voyage and could not decide how to go. By steamship would be faster and infinitely more comfortable, but also much more expensive than by merchantman. She borrowed some money from the Marchesa Arconati, more from a bank, giving Marcus Spring's name as security. But still there would not be enough for passage by steamship.

With her friends the Moziers, who knew the captain, she went to inspect a freighter, the *Elizabeth*, docked at Livorno. She discovered that Captain Seth Hasty was a staunch Yankee who had sailed the seas for many years. His wife, Catherine, was with him on this voyage. Margaret liked them at once and liked the trim four-masted vessel that looked small but both clean and sturdy. The merchantman was taking on a cargo of silk, olive oil, almonds, old paintings, and 150 tons of Carrara marble. All seemed propitious and Margaret signed for the long voyage to New York.

Still, she was apprehensive. Friends in Florence tried to dissuade her. They pointed out that sixty or seventy days on such a small ship would seem endless.

There would be no doctor aboard. What if one of them fell ill? The cabin, being on the open deck, would be at the mercy of gale winds and pounding waves. They would have to take their own provisions, even a cow or a goat for little Angelo's milk. Didn't Margaret remember how she had suffered from seasickness on that fast, safe voyage from Boston to Liverpool?

Margaret remembered. She herself was full of anxiety. But this time she wasn't afraid for herself. She admitted she was a coward for Angelino's sake, and for her husband's, because he had never been aboard a ship. She prayed that nothing would happen to them. If it did, she hoped it would happen to all of them. She would not want to survive without her husband and her son.

When they went aboard in the early morning of May 17, 1850, the weather was perfect: the breeze was brisk, the sun bright, and both sky and sea were the incomparable blue of a spring morning on the Mediterranean.

The passenger list was small. Besides the captain's wife and the Ossolis, there were only two others—a young Italian girl, Celeste Paolini, going to work in New York as a domestic, who had agreed to help look after Angelino on the voyage, and a young American friend and devotee of Margaret's from the old days of

Brook Farm, Horace Sumner. He had spent the winter in Florence for his health but said that he had come also "to see cathedrals and Margaret." He and Ossoli were congenial; they planned to exchange English and Italian lessons.

Angelino quickly became everyone's favorite. He crowed with delight over everything—the billowing white sails, the raucous cry of the sea birds, the other boats, large and small, that they passed on their way to Gibraltar, and the white, shaggy goat that had been brought aboard for his milk supply. The sailors romped with the boy, and when the captain was off duty, he took the boy up on his lap and told him stories. Margaret was seasick but did not mind very much, knowing that her son was well taken care of.

Then the blow fell. Captain Hasty became very ill, was in agony for days with a painful rash, a hacking cough, and a throat so swollen that he could not speak and scarcely could swallow. As soon as they anchored off Gibraltar, Mrs. Hasty tried to send for a doctor, but it was too late. The rugged Yankee captain died of smallpox. The ship was put under quarantine for a week; no one was allowed to board her or leave her. The good captain was buried at sea on a beautiful Sunday morning. All the flags in the harbor were flown at half-mast. Margaret tried to comfort Mrs. Hasty.

As they set sail again, under Mr. Bangs, the new, less-experienced navigator, she worried about little Angelino; and her worries soon turned to anguish when the child, too, broke out with all the frightening symptoms of smallpox. His eyes were swollen shut, his face ballooned out of shape, his body erupted with sores. Once again the parents hovered over him, applying soothing poultices, offering spoonfuls of cooling liquids. Thanks to their tireless efforts and probably, too, to the vaccine he had been given as an infant, Angelino recovered. The whole ship rejoiced when once again he could play out on deck with his friends the sailors.

There was smooth sailing for the rest of the long voyage. Margaret added to and reworked parts of her History. Ossoli and she walked round and round the deck together under the stars. He and the youthful Sumner resumed their language lessons. Celeste, the young Italian girl, helped take care of the child and, between times, dreamed of her new life in America. Mrs. Hasty and Margaret had long talks together.

Finally, on July 19, off the New Jersey coast, all cheered Mr. Bangs when he announced that they would land the next day in New York. Trunks were brought up from the hold and were packed. Margaret chose the hand-embroidered frock the child would wear next day when he would first set foot on the soil of his mother's native land. After cheery good nights, the passengers retired to their staterooms.

The storm that began about nine o'clock became a hurricane by midnight, and at four in the morning drove the *Elizabeth* off course and headlong into a sand bar off Fire Island. The terrific jarring shook the ship, tossed the passengers from their berths, and caused chaos everywhere, from the bow stuck deep in the sand to the stern swinging wildly and helplessly in the waves. The heavy marble broke through her bottom, and water rushed into the hold. Mountainous waves poured over the decks, the skylight of the cabin was smashed, and water like a Niagara descended, dousing the lights.

Margaret in her long white nightgown snatched up Angelino, wrapped a blanket about him, and blindly followed Ossoli, who guided them all to the temporary protection of the windward cabin walls, where for a time they could brace themselves against a heavy table.

The little boy cried in fright. Celeste sobbed. Margaret held Angelino close and crooned a lullaby. Ossoli prayed with Celeste until she quieted. Mrs. Hasty and Sumner clasped hands to give each other courage. Around them all was awash—broken glass, trunks, pieces of timber, everything that was loose being swept in and out the fallen doorway.

Mr. Davis, the mate, with the help of two sailors, finally succeeded in half carrying, half dragging the passengers to the less-exposed forecastle. Angelino was carried there in a canvas bag slung around the neck of a brawny sailor. The mate risked his life twice again to fetch for Mrs. Hasty her husband's gold watch, for Margaret some of her money, and for all of them some wine and figs.

Margaret, remembering her abandoned History, said quietly to Mrs. Hasty, "There still remains what, if I live, will be of more value to me than anything." But she could not bring herself to ask Mr. Davis to risk his life again.

With daylight, through the rain, they could see people gathering on shore, and hoped for rescue. But none came. Their own lifeboats had been washed overboard and swept out to sea. The men on the beach were there to seize valuables that were washed ashore, not to help people.

The remaining hours were a nightmare. In attempting to swim to shore, one or two sailors made it, one or two drowned. Sumner, who plunged into the waves, was lost. Davis proposed that each passenger should ride a plank, grasping handles of a rope, being guided by a sailor swimming behind. Mrs. Hasty volunteered to try it first. She made it, though she briefly disappeared twice under the waves and no one on the ship could see whether or not she reached the shore. Margaret steadfastly refused to go without Ossoli and the baby, still hoping that the three of them could somehow be rescued together. A lifeboat did finally appear on shore, but no one would venture forth in it in the mountainous waves.

When in midafternoon the tide began to rise again, the few left on board knew that now was their last chance. The steward took baby Angelino in his arms and plunged into the water. A heavy swell struck the forecastle, the foremast fell, the deck and all on it were washed away. Celeste, Ossoli, and last of all Margaret sank beneath the waves. They were never found. The steward and the baby were found dead, their bodies washed up on the beach.

Margaret's History was lost. She had said she would return "possessed of a great history." She had returned, but the history she left to the world was that of herself, the history of Margaret Fuller—bluestocking, romantic, revolutionary—a woman of the nineteenth century.

Bibliography

Alcott, Louisa May: *Transcendental Wild Oats*. Harvard,
Mass.: The Harvard Common Press, 1975.

Anthony, Katherine: *Margaret Fuller: A Psychological
Biography*. Boston: Harcourt Brace & Howe, 1920.

Bell, Margaret: *Margaret Fuller*. Introduction by Mrs.
Franklin D. Roosevelt. N.Y.: Charles Boni, 1930.

Berkeley, G. F. H. & J.: *Italy in the Making: June 1846
to January 1848*. England: Cambridge University
Press, 1936.

———: *Italy in the Making: January 1st to November
16th, 1848*. England: Cambridge University Press,
1940.

Bradford, Gamaliel: *Portraits of American Women*. Boston: Houghton, 1919.

Brooks, Van Wyck: *The Flowering of New England*. N.Y.: Dutton, 1936.

————: *The Life of Emerson*. N.Y.: Dutton, 1932.

Cabot, James Elliot: *A Memoir of Ralph Waldo Emerson*, Vol. I. Boston: Houghton, Mifflin, 1887.

Chipperfield, Faith: *In Quest of Love*. N.Y.: Coward-McCann, 1957.

Conroy, Virginia: "Margaret Fuller, 19th Century Women's Liberator," *Rhode Island Yearbook*, R.I., 1971.

Deiss, Joseph Jay: *The Roman Years of Margaret Fuller*. N.Y.: Crowell, 1969.

Durning, Russell E.: *Margaret Fuller: Citizen of the World*. Heidelberg, 1969.

Eakin, Paul John: "Margaret Fuller, Hawthorne, James and Sexual Politics," *South Atlantic Quarterly*, vol. 75. Summer, 1976.

Emerson, Edward Waldo & Forbes, W. E.: *Journals of Ralph W. Emerson*. Boston: Houghton, Mifflin, 1910.

Greeley, Horace: *Recollections of a Busy Life*, Vol. I. Port Washington, N.Y.: Kennikat Press, 1971.

Hawthorne, Nathaniel: *Blithedale Romance*. Boston: Ticknor & Fields, 1859.

Hibbert, Christopher: *Garibaldi and His Enemies*. London: Longmans, Green, 1965.

Higginson, Thomas Wentworth: *Margaret Fuller Ossoli*. N.Y.: Haskell House, 1968.

Howe, Julia Ward: *Reminiscences*. Boston/N.Y.: Houghton, Mifflin, 1899.

James, Henry: *The Bostonians*, Vols. I & II. N.Y.: Macmillan, 1921.

————: *William Wetmore Story and His Friends*. N.Y.: Grove Press, 1957.

Lowell, James Russell: *A Fable for Critics*. N.Y.: Putnam, 1848.

MacPhail, Andrew: *Essays on Puritanism*. Boston: Houghton, Mifflin, 1905.

Martineau, Harriet: *Society in America*. N.Y.: Saunders & Otley, 1837.

————: *Autobiography*. Ed. by Maria Weston Chapman. Boston: J. R. Osgood, 1877.

Maurois, André: *Lélia: The Life of George Sand*. Trans. by Gerard Hopkins. N.Y.: Harper, 1953.

Miller, Perry, ed.: *Margaret Fuller—American Romantic: A Selection from Her Writings and Correspondence*. Garden City, N.Y.: Anchor Books, Doubleday, 1963.

Morison, Samuel Eliot. *Three Centuries of Harvard*. Cambridge, Mass.: Harvard University Press, 1936.

Ossoli, Margaret Fuller: *Love-Letters of Margaret Fuller, 1845–1846*. Introduction by Julia Ward Howe. To which are added *The Reminiscences of Ralph Waldo Emerson, Horace Greeley and Charles T. Congdon*. N.Y.: Greenwood Press, 1969.

————: *Life Without and Life Within*. Ed. by her brother, Arthur B. Fuller. Boston: Roberts Brothers, 1875.

————: *At Home and Abroad, or Things and Thoughts in America and Europe*. Ed. by her brother, Arthur B. Fuller. Port Washington, N.Y.: Kennikat Press, 1971.

Ossoli, Sarah Margaret (Fuller) Marchesa d': *1810–1850: Memoirs of Margaret Fuller Ossoli.* Ed. by Ralph Waldo Emerson, William Henry Channing, James Freeman Clarke. Reprint of the 1884 edition. N.Y.: Lenox Hill, 1972. Vols I & II.

Parrington, V. L.: *Main Currents of American Thought,* Vol. II: *The Romantic Revolution.* N.Y.: Harcourt Brace, 1958.

Perry, Bliss, ed.: *The Heart of Emerson's Journals.* Cambridge, Mass.: The Riverside Press, 1926.

Quennell, Peter: "The Odd Couple," *Horizon,* vol. 18, No. 3, pp. 98–106. Summer, 1976.

Shapiro, Fred C.: "The Transcending Margaret Fuller." *Ms,* November 1972.

Stern, Madeleine B.: *The Life of Margaret Fuller.* N.Y.: Haskell House, 1942.

Story, William Wetmore: *Roba di Roma.* London: Chapman and Hall, 1875.

Vaillant, General: *Le Siège de Rome en 1849.* Paris, 1851.

Wade, Mason: *Margaret Fuller: Whetstone of Genius.* N.Y.: Viking, 1940.

————: *The Writings of Margaret Fuller.* N.Y.: Viking, 1941.

Wilson, David Alec: *Carlyle on Cromwell and Others (1837–48).* N.Y.: Dutton, 1925.

Index

Emerson, Lidian, 49, 52
Emerson, Ralph Waldo, 70, 71, 76, 98; sermons and lectures of, 39, 58; becomes Margaret's friend, 49; Margaret's visits to, 52–4, 105; and Alcott, 57; and Green St. Academy, 61; Margaret's letters to and from, 62, 146; recommendation of Margaret by, 63, 116; and *Dial*, 67–8; and Margaret's job on *Tribune*, 80

Emerson, Waldo, 54
England, poverty in, 115
Europe, Margaret to, 99, 101–3; *see also names of cities and countries in*

Fable for Critics, 85
Farrar, Mr. and Mrs. John, 35, 37–9, 43–5, 48–9
Fishkill, 79
Florence, Margaret to, 137, 140, 166–71
French Revolution, The, 115
Fuller, Abraham, 47–8, 143
Fuller, Arthur, 33, 40
Fuller, Ellen, 33, 40, 48, 73; and Ellery Channing, 70, 146
Fuller, Eugene, 33, 40, 48, 146
Fuller, Colonel Hiram, 60–1
Fuller, Lloyd, 40
Fuller, Margaret Crane, 5, 8, 12, 41; gentleness of, 4, 11; and Adams party, 32–3; nurses Margaret, 43; and husband's death, 46,

48; sells farm, 63; visits children, 73, 82, 98; and Margaret's New York job, 82; worries about Margaret, 146; Margaret's letters to, 152, 160–1, 164–5; and Margaret's marriage, 166–7

Fuller, Richard, 33, 40, 146
Fuller, Sarah Margaret, birth of, 3; and books, 4–9, 12–13, 27, 30, 37, 58; education and childhood of, 4–9, 12–13, 15–29; becomes Margaret, 10–11; brothers and sister of, 11–12, 33, 40, 47–8, 70, 73, 146; special friends of, 15–16, 35, 37–9, 43–5, 49, 72; and sympathetic teacher, 24–6, 28–9; studies Greek, 27–9; social development of, 30–5, 37; journal of, 36, 42, 46, 71, 76, 82, 107, 112, 141–2; and Goethe, 37, 58, 60, 62; and American history, 41–2; first published writing of, 42; illness of, 43, 58, 69, 94, 103, 139, 144–5, 173; becomes teacher, 54, 56–8, 60–2; and education for women, 64; as editor, 67–9; and women's rights, 69, 80, 86–7; and marriage, 71, 86, 136, 142–3, 163–4, 167; pregnancy and birth of child of, 142–9; and return to America, 170–7; writings

Martineau, Harriet, 43, 48–9, 105–6
Mazzini, Giuseppe, 118–20, 127, 131, 133, 156–8, 162, 166
Mechanics' Institutes, 104
Monroe, James, 6
Mount Holyoke, 63
Mozier, Mr. and Mrs. Joseph, 140, 171
"Murders in the Rue Morgue, The," 85

Napoleon, Louis, 157
Nathan, James, 88–103, 104, 106–8, 147
New York, Margaret to, 71, 80, 82–101
New York *Tribune*, Margaret offered job on, 71, 78; Margaret's work on, 84–5, 88, 97; and Margaret's book, 87; Nathan's articles in, 95, 98, 101; Margaret's foreign articles to, 99, 104, 115, 120, 128, 137, 140, 154–5; and George Sand, 126; and Margaret's pregnancy, 141–51; Margaret dropped from, 167
Niagara Falls, 73
North American Review, 41

Ossoli, Angelo Eugenio Filippo, 170; birth of, 149–50; and smallpox, 151, 174; baptism of, 151–2; in Rieti, 155–6, 159–62;

illness of, 162–3; and grandmother, 164–6; and *Elizabeth*, 172–7
Ossoli, Giovanni Angelo, helps Margaret, 129–30; tells Margaret life story, 130–1; and united Italy, 131, 133, 134, 137, 140, 142–3, 162; second meeting with Margaret, 132–3; love of, for Margaret, 134, 137–8, 140–1, 145, 147, 165; proposes marriage, 136–7; and Margaret's pregnancy, 142–3, 146–9; and Civil Guard, 142, 147, 148, 153, 155; and son, 149–52, 155, 163; meets Mazzini, 157; and war, 159–61; marries Margaret, 164–5; and Margaret's mother, 165–6; and surveillance, 170; on board *Elizabeth*, 172–7
Oudinot, General Nicolas, 157–8

Paolini, Celeste, 172, 174, 175, 177
Paris, Margaret to, 120, 122–7; poverty in, 123
Park, Dr., academy, Margaret at, 12–13
Peabody, Elizabeth, 65
Perkins, Mr., school of, 27–9
Philadelphia *Gazette*, 68
Pilgrim's Progress, The, 166
Pius IX, Pope, 129, 133, 134, 148, 153–4, 156–8, 166
Poe, Edgar Allan, 85